Selecting College and University Personnel:
The Quest and the Questions

by Richard A. Kaplowitz

ASHE-ERIC Higher Education Report No. 8, 1986

Prepared by

 ® *Clearinghouse on Higher Education*
The George Washington University

Published by

Association for the Study of Higher Education

Jonathan D. Fife,
Series Editor

Cite as
Kaplowitz, Richard A. *Selecting College and University Personnel: The Quest and the Questions*. ASHE-ERIC Higher Education Report No. 8. Washington, D.C.: Association for the Study of Higher Education, 1986.

Cover design by Michael David Brown, Inc., Rockville, MD.

The ERIC Clearinghouse on Higher Education invites individuals to submit proposals for writing monographs for the Higher Education Report series. Proposals must include:
1. A detailed manuscript proposal of not more than five pages.
2. A 75-word summary to be used by several review committees for the initial screening and rating of each proposal.
3. A vita.
4. A writing sample.

Library of Congress Catalog Card Number 86-70537
ISSN 0884-0040
ISBN 0-913317-35-7

ERIC° Clearinghouse on Higher Education
The George Washington University
One Dupont Circle, Suite 630
Washington, D.C. 20036

ASHE Association for the Study of Higher Education
One Dupont Circle, Suite 630
Washington, D.C. 20036

Office of Educational
Research and Improvement
U.S. Department of Education

This publication was partially prepared with funding from the Office of Educational Research and Improvement, U.S. Department of Education, under contract no. 400-86-0017. The opinions expressed in this report do not necessarily reflect the positions or policies of OERI or the Department.

EXECUTIVE SUMMARY

The selection of the faculty and the administrative leadership on campus is at the very heart of the future of the academic enterprise. Institutions seek to recruit and hire the finest people possible, and the selection processes used include many elements of the monomythical quest or journey. The use of the search committee in the selection of campus leaders has evolved into an almost hallowed approach. Additionally, consultants are now providing support and assistance in recruitment on a number of campuses. Findings about the search committee process include many positive elements. Procedural and societal issues, however, need to be addressed so that the potential pitfalls can be avoided while the best candidates are found.

What Helps Search Committees Function Well?

The number of ways to increase the likelihood of an effective search include:

1. The process is highly politicized, particularly at the presidential level. Be sure that search committee members are constituency-inclusive.
2. Search committee dynamics can be superlative or bitter. Trust and open communications among committee members are important contributors to a positive environment and may need direct focus and attention.
3. There is no perfect candidate or perfect position; further, a superb candidate for one campus in one situation might be a disaster on another. It is important to delineate the particular needs of the campus (for the next five years at the very least) at the time of the search in order to determine the kind of leadership needed.
4. Actively seek candidates, including those who may be happily employed elsewhere. Good networking skills combined with effective and affirmative outreach are necessary in order to generate a good candidate pool.
5. Consultants are used more than in the past. A range of providers of consulting services is available. Consultants are most helpful in three ways: structuring the search, locating good candidates, and checking references. If consultants are to be used, make that decision early in the process.
6. Good candidates are lost when confidentiality is breached or absent; take steps throughout the process to assure that confidentiality is maintained.

7. Faculty salary inequities arise from the non-academic marketplace. Salary inequities raise issues of comparable worth and of fairness. These issues need to be resolved internally on campus, so that differences generated by them do not end up expressed as hostility focused on candidates for positions.

8. Women are gaining in numbers of administrative appointments; minority group members are not; further, the long-term pool of minority candidates has started decreasing. Extra efforts are needed to maintain these initial successes of women, and to increase the development of minority group members. Effective affirmative action programs help.

9. The Supreme Court strongly upholds affirmative action; the Executive Branch, under its current leadership, does not.

10. True sensitivity to and concern for people may be the prime attributes of leadership; looking for these traits appears more important than particular degrees or publications.

11. Checking references requires maintaining confidentiality while securing accurate information; proceed with caution. Reference checks are important to determine whether a candidate has the necessary strength and courage to reach out, to survive some failures, and to keep trying, without ever losing sight of the individual people who are the most important part of any organization.

12. Interviews assess sociability and verbal fluency but don't predict administrative success. When a candidate is invited to a campus for an interview, in-depth, two-way interviewing is important if the selection is to be based on the qualities needed for that campus rather than on a slick or showy style. In an interview, learning why a candidate took a particular course of action is more revealing than what was done.

13. Personnel offices provide helpful support services in academic searches; make use of them.

14. Remember that candidates are vulnerable to the process that focuses so much energy and attention on them; be caring and thoughtful.

Why is Confidentiality So Important?
Confidentiality is important in order to secure the very
strongest possible candidates in a search. Search committees tend to look more for proven competence than for
potential, particularly when seeking to fill a high-level
vacancy. Most people with proven competence already are
at work and most often that work involves sensitive political relationships. Some of those people may be willing to
consider a move. But, while they are employed elsewhere,
they are unwilling to take a chance on eroding their effectiveness on their current campuses.

The folklore, and now even a good bit of the literature, is
replete with horror stories of candidates whose interest in a
position became known on the home campus with sometimes quite negative results; candidates know those stories,
and they are reluctant to risk having their careers jeopar-
dized in like manner. McLaughlin and Riesman have
focused significant attention on this issue.

What Societal Issues Need Attention?
Two larger societal issues also need to be addressed. One
relates to open meeting laws, and the other to the result of
apparent social inequities. Clear evidence reveals that
many good candidates are withdrawing from, or not even
allowing their names to be considered in, high level
searches in states which search "in the sunshine." The
old, secret ways of doing business too often were not in the
best interests of the public. Sunshine laws are clearly
intended to be, and for the most part very much are, in the
public interest. However, good leadership from within
public higher education, working with other comparably
concerned public agencies, needs to seek legislative re-
examination of that aspect of sunshine laws that requires
the public listing of candidates and public discussions
about the professional and personal reputations of those
candidates.

Second, there is a need for multiphasic attention to
actively develop the talent and abilities that are not adequately coming to maturation in our minority populations.
If we are to have a broadly constituted faculty in 20 years,
now is the time to increase broadly based social efforts to
reach and nurture that future faculty.

ADVISORY BOARD

CONSULTING EDITORS

Paul A. Albrecht
Executive Vice President and Dean
Claremont Graduate School

G. Lester Anderson
Professor Emeritus
Pennsylvania State University

Robert C. Andringa
President
Creative Solutions

John B. Bennett
Director, Office on Self-Regulation
American Council on Education

Carole J. Bland
Associate Professor, Family Practice and Community Health
University of Minnesota

L. Leon Campbell
Provost and Vice President for Academic Affairs
University of Delaware

Judith A. Clementson-Mohr
Director of Psychological Services
Purdue University

Mark H. Curtis
President Emeritus
Association of American Colleges

Martin Finkelstein
Associate Professor of Higher Education Administration
Seton Hall University

Andrew T. Ford
Provost and Dean of College
Allegheny College

Roderick S. French
Vice President for Academic Affairs
George Washington University

Timothy Gallineau
Vice President for Student Development
Saint Bonaventure University

Milton Greenberg
Provost
American University

James C. Hearn
Associate Professor, Educational Policy and Administration
University of Minnesota

Jules B. LaPidus
President
Council of Graduate Schools in the United States

Theodore J. Marchese
Vice President
American Association for Higher Education

Arthur S. Marmaduke
Director
Eureka Project

John D. Marshall
Assistant to the Executive Vice President and Provost
Georgia State University

Judith B. McLaughlin
Research Associate on Education and Sociology
Harvard University

Richard M. Millard
President
Council on Postsecondary Accreditation

L. Jackson Newell
Professor and Dean
University of Utah

Steven G. Olswang
Assistant Provost for Academic Affairs
University of Washington

Thomas J. Quatroche
Professor and Chair, Educational Foundations Department
State University College at Buffalo

S. Andrew Schaffer
Vice President and General Counsel
New York University

John P. Sciacca
Assistant Professor, Health, Physical Education, and Recreation
Northern Arizona University

Thomas R. Wolanin
Staff Director, Subcommittee on Postsecondary Education
United States House of Representatives

CONTENTS

FOREWORD

The issue of selecting competent personnel reminds me of a conversation I had with a senior colleague recently. He was bemoaning how hiring practices had changed in recent times. "In the old days, it was easy," he explained to me. "We always invited our old friends to the campus. Those who were able to walk across the campus pond were interviewed." While the hope of finding a person of super-human capabilities has not changed, the practice of tapping into the closed network of friends and acquaintances—the so-called "old boys' club"—is no longer tolerated.

This report, with the apt subtitle of "The Quest and the Questions," could also be called "The Myths and the Realities." While the desire to continue to do things as they were done in the past may still be strong, many past practices do not meet the strict rules of accountability and acceptability that are needed today. Hiring practices are further complicated by considerations that are external to the traditional borders of the campus. For example, colleges and universities must now compete with industry for talented scholars and researchers, which in the process drives salaries upward.

The value placed on openness, as evidenced by sunshine laws, conflicts with the need for confidentiality. The recognized benefits of equal opportunity and affirmative action further necessitate the need for being proactive in filling positions.

As external pressures have increased, techniques in the personnel selection process have also changed. Collegial networks, bolstered by the ever-growing professional associations and annual conferences, have never been wider. Job announcements, carried in popular press as well as trade newspapers, have never received more exposure. Never before has the business of running higher education institutions been so closely observed. Demands for accountability have called for wider representation in the selection process, especially on search committees. Recognition of the complexity of personnel selection has led to the appearance of a new breed of consultants on campuses, the professional headhunters.

Indeed, the author of this monograph is himself of this new breed. Richard Kaplowitz, when he is not tending to his duties as dean of the college at the New England Institute of Applied Arts and Sciences, is the president of

TEEM, Inc., a consulting firm offering a variety of services, including personnel training and evaluation. In this report, he offers a comprehensive review of the literature available on selecting competent personnel. He offers specific advice on such common procedures as forming and running a search committee, qualities to look for in a candidate, how to conduct a useful interview, and how to get worthwhile references.

For most of us, selecting new personnel is a duty as distasteful as it is necessary. It is time-consuming, sometimes unrewarding, and difficult. Yet is is one of the most vital functions of any successful institution. This report will help chief personnel officers and search committee participants to understand how to make the best use of their time and energy. The difference can be between getting the right candidate and reconstituting the committee all too soon again for another try.

Jonathan D. Fife
Series Editor
Professor and Director
ERIC Clearinghouse on Higher Education
The George Washington University

ACKNOWLEDGMENTS

It is true indeed that some things need to be believed to be seen. I am most grateful to those nutritious friends—beginning with Lisette, Dave, and Rob—whose support, help, and encouragement keep me sane and happy; they believed in this book.

I also would like to express my appreciation to:

- those colleagues who so willingly shared their professional knowledge, expertise, research, and trade secrets, including most particularly David Riesman and Judith Block McLaughlin for their very graciously extended sense of common purpose;
- my colleagues at New England Institute of Applied Arts and Sciences, who kept the campus operating well while I was writing;
- Mark, Nancy, and Rob, who helped in the final stages of manuscript production;
- my editor and special friend, Lisette.

Contrary to the ancient myth, wisdom does not burst forth fully developed . . . it is built up, small step by small step, from most irrational beginnings (Bettelheim 1977, p. 5).

The selection of academic personnel and particularly of academic leadership often conveys a sense of the mythical and mystical.

Asked to consider the search and selection process in higher education, Jungian analysts might suggest that search committees and candidates alike follow the path of a mythical journey or quest. The steps on this path include:

- A call is heard;
- A decision is made to heed the call, to make the journey;
- Trials are encountered and faced;
- Often a dark, no-progress stage (being stuck "in the belly of the whale") is encountered;
- Progress is made and problems are solved, generally with the help of allies and nutritious friends;
- The treasure is gained;
- A magic flight back to one's own land completes the journey (Campbell 1968).

The selection of academic personnel and particularly of academic leadership often conveys a sense of the mythical and mystical. The search committee goes through an elaborate quest, each candidate undertakes an elaborate journey, and the end result for each is, hopefully, the addition of a unique treasure to the real world of the particular college campus. The desired result certainly will meet one characteristic element of each mythical tale, that "this is absolutely unique; it could not have happened to any other person, or in any other setting" (Bettelheim 1977, p. 36).

In the 14 years since the American Council on Education's handbook on selecting academic administrators was published (Kaplowitz 1973), many articles, a number of doctoral dissertations, and several books have been written on various aspects of the search and selection process. This literature has focused on, elaborated upon, and reported research related to the various steps in the process. It has provided current information on legal and procedural aspects of interviewing and appointments. And it has developed a context for the patterns of seeking and

---

selecting academic personnel in the late 1980s and into the 1990s.

The following review of the available literature is designed to assist in the quest by reporting the current wisdom, practices, and findings, and by helping each person involved in a search and selection process formulate the questions that must be answered in order to gain, as an ultimate treasure or end goal, administrators and faculty members who will steadily focus on asking, ''How does this or that make us a better place to learn?'' (Healy 1985, p. 22).

In order to seek widely for the best wisdom available, three main categories of sources have been used. The primary source is the literature of higher education. A second arena for review is suggested by the assertion that:

> *The administration of higher education is increasingly taking on the characteristics of corporate management . . . Personnel decision making has become more formal and more centralized on campuses across the country . . . [Increasingly], professional employees have . . . come under the influence of the personnel office* (Kemerer, Mensel, and Baldridge 1981, p. 17).

Selected literature from the corporate and industrial personnel field, therefore, also is drawn upon in this review.

The third source is somewhat more amorphous—those formal and informal conversations, at professional meetings and by telephone, with colleagues who are personnel practitioners and consultants. These conversations yield some of the most basic realities and data of current practice. Some colleagues have published their findings, and their writings are cited. In other cases, people who deal with some of the very sensitive issues of personnel selection and placement have spoken freely only with the knowledge that their comments will not be formally attributed to them.

Following is a review and discussion of

- *The steps of the search process,* with separate chapters on administrative and faculty selection;
- *Some major issues within that process,* including the emergence and use of search consultants, confidentiality vs. open searches, and affirmative action;

- *Specific aspects of the search,* including administrative position requirements, securing useful and accurate references, and interviewing candidates effectively.

A brief look at the personnel office on campus concludes this work.

THE SEARCH PROCESS

The Selection of Administrators

Searches for college and university personnel include searches for administrators, for faculty members, and for non-academic support staff members. This chapter will review and discuss the steps in the search and selection process that is used primarily for the recruitment of administrative personnel. Subsequent chapters will address particular aspects and issues of faculty recruitment and the recruitment of support personnel.

In presidential and academic administrative searches, the use of a search committee has become just about unquestioned.

> *Whatever the ideal procedure may be, for most institutions the first step is the appointment of a search and selection committee or committees* (Nason 1980, p. 15).

The perceived campus need for politically legitimated appointments appears to be a paramount factor in the centrality of the search committee in the process; additionally, the primacy of the search committee comes from the recognition of both the volume of work done by committee members and the collective wisdom that a good committee can bring to the enterprise. Consultants sometimes are employed to support and assist search committees.

A recent study began with the hypothesis "that universities have been unable to recruit and hire their first-choice candidate for a position" (Rodman and Dingerson 1986, p. 25). Their findings, to the contrary, were that in 123 searches for academic deans, 84.6 percent reported that they were able to hire their first-choice candidate. (There are some observers who would cite that result as further evidence of their contention that search committees come together around the candidate who represents the lowest common denominator.)

When administrators are sought in such areas as finance and institutional advancement, outside consultants working with presidents more often may be engaged to recruit, screen, and identify several or one key nominee for a vacancy. At that point, the candidate(s) in question most often will be invited to visit the campus, both to help sell the job to the candidate, and for a test of chemistry with key campus personnel. Such visits tend to have very differ-

ent overtones and undertones than do visits emerging from the work of search committees.

Quite frequently a vacancy occurs without the luxury of six to nine months advance notice. Normally, an acting administrator is appointed to fill the position in the interim. De Zonia suggests that, where possible, "the board should consider the desirability of appointing a non-candidate . . . as acting" (1979, p. 34). Nason more strongly asserts that acting presidents can come from inside or outside the institution, with "one absolutely essential condition being that he or she is in no way a candidate for the permanent position" (1980, p. 14).

Campus realities, however, quite often reveal cases where an "acting" administrator is appointed with every expectation that the "acting" ultimately will be the appointee. Search committees generally are convened even in these cases; faculty cynicism can (legitimately) abound in what seem likely to be "wired" searches. In at least one such case, however, the slowness with which a reluctant search committee got itself organized and under way allowed the acting dean enough time to alienate totally both her faculty and the upper-level administration in the university, and to lose the "sure" appointment to an outside candidate.

The importance of avoiding both the appearance and the reality of predetermined searches, and the negative feelings and institutional images that can result from involving outside candidates in such situations, are noted frequently (Bisesi 1985; Felicetti 1984; Kaplowitz 1973). Campuses get mixed guidance when exploring the issues which surface when strong internal candidates exist. One perspective states:

> *Every effort should be made to find someone already on campus for the job. No external names should be solicited, much less screened, until the committee has exhausted all internal possibilities. The presidency should be posted internally like any other job opening. The committee should solicit nominations and pursue whatever in-house names emerge. Only if the internal possibilities are unacceptable should the committee advertise and actively recruit names (Bisesi 1985, p. 23).*

An alternative perspective recommends:

Even when there is a strong, obvious internal candidate for an administrative position, a [full] search is heartily recommended. If the internal candidate is selected after the search, the mandate accompanying that selection is much more convincing than it would have been without a search. On the other hand, promising internal candidates might not seem so strong when compared with external candidates who may be uncovered by the search process. Search committees must, of course, be sure that the search process is honestly and thoroughly conducted once begun (Kaplowitz 1973, p. 2).

A topic frequently discussed, yet seldom researched, is the rationale underlying decisions that are made on whether an inside or an outside candidate is preferable:

- One sometimes helpful and simple construct is that when things have been going well and in desired directions on a campus or in a subunit thereof, leadership from inside may be sought more often; when a change in direction is needed, an outsider may appear more desirable.
- A second hypothesis, which seems partially supported by the research, is that internal candidates for president are less likely to be successful than are inside candidates for provost and dean. It can be suggested that the president needs to arrive unencumbered politically, while the faculty may be most comfortable with an academic leader who knows the culture of the particular campus and who has earned the trust of colleagues over years of shared service.
- One further note is that people who are or have previously served as presidents often seem to be preferred candidates for the presidency. It may be easier for board members to imagine someone as a president who already has held that title, and who has done the job, whether it was done well or otherwise. Those candidates usually are outside.

Any and all of these concepts, however, easily are confounded in light of the specifics of the personalities and political affiliations of the available internal and external candidates and of the appointing boards and officers as well.

Both Nason (1980) and Perry (1984) point out that industry trains and develops executive successors and promotes heavily from within, while academia does not. Noting that only about 30 percent of college and university presidents are appointed from within, and 70 percent from outside of the institution, Perry says that in higher education:

This decided preference to go outside for new presidents is primarily due to academe's emphasis on the participatory management style . . . [which] . . . does not . . . encourage the development of a strong executive succession system (1984, p. 215).

Along similar lines, in their study of 110 searches for academic deans, Rodman and Dingerson (1986) found that 35.5 percent were filled by internal candidates, and 64.5 percent were filled by external candidates. 1986 research data being analyzed by Moden and Miller of Ohio University suggests that about half of chief academic officers are selected from within their institutions. Further research on the rationale for preferring an inside or an outside candidate would be useful.

Steps in the Search and Selection Process
The search process can be divided into a series of somewhat overlapping stages. Kauffman (1974, p. 33) identifies six objectives to be met in order for a search committee to be able to submit a list of recommendations from which the board will select the next president. Libby (1983) discusses nine steps in community college presidential selection. Kaplowitz (1973, p. 10) delineates 24 steps in eight phases in the search for academic administrators. The flow chart provides a sequential summary of those steps (see figure 1).

Nason (1980, 1984) divides presidential selection and appointment into nine major steps with eight checklists provided to help assure that each step has been properly accomplished. Those steps include:

1. establishing the machinery of search and selection;

2. *organizing the committee, including the role of the person chairing the committee, staffing, and office needs;*
3. *formulating the criteria;*
4. *selecting the pool of candidates;*
5. *screening candidates;*
6. *interviewing candidates;*
7. *selecting top candidates;*
8. *appointing the president;*
9. *reporting and transition planning.*

These stages provide a context for additional discussion in those arenas where current issues and concerns transcend or supersede the basic listing of steps to be taken.

Organizational Tasks for the Committee
A key issue in starting the search process is the delineation of the needs of the institution. Without losing too much momentum by becoming trapped in a "paralysis of analysis," it is important to take sufficient time to identify those abilities and attributes that will be necessary for success over the next five (for presidents, perhaps ten) years for the person who will be selected to fill the post.

Statements of 'desired qualifications' are usually general wish lists. It is up to the board to identify the strengths ·and capabilities most important to the institution at the present time (Kaffer 1981, p. 16).

One approach is to "begin with an evaluation of the issues that will be facing the new administrator and an outline of the campus's strengths and weaknesses." And, as "no person has done everything that everyone wants in an administrator," a set of "preferred" attributes is suggested (Bisesi 1985, p. 22). In some cases, it may be appropriate to "sound out the constituencies" to ascertain an institution's current needs (Strider 1981, p. 32). Requirements viewed as necessary for success in particular administrative roles are discussed in the chapter on administrative attributes.

The listing of abilities and attributes can be undertaken by the trustees when seeking a president or by the president or other supervisor for other administrators. Alterna-

A key issue in starting the search process is the delineation of the needs of the institution.

FIGURE 1
THE SEARCH PROCESS

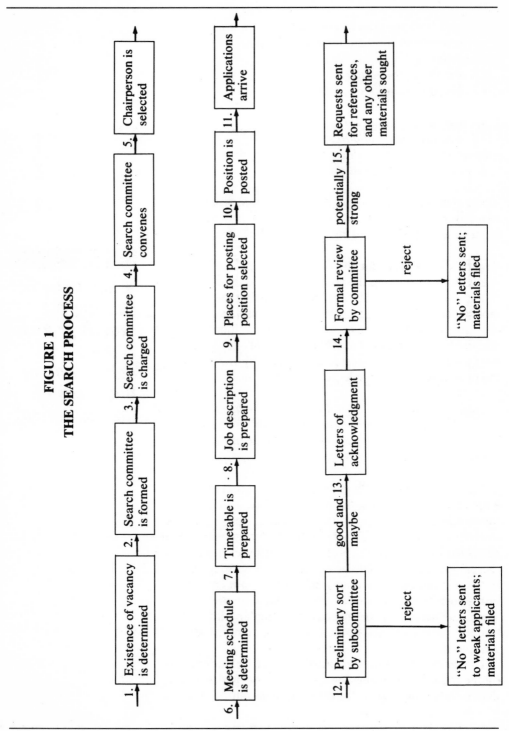

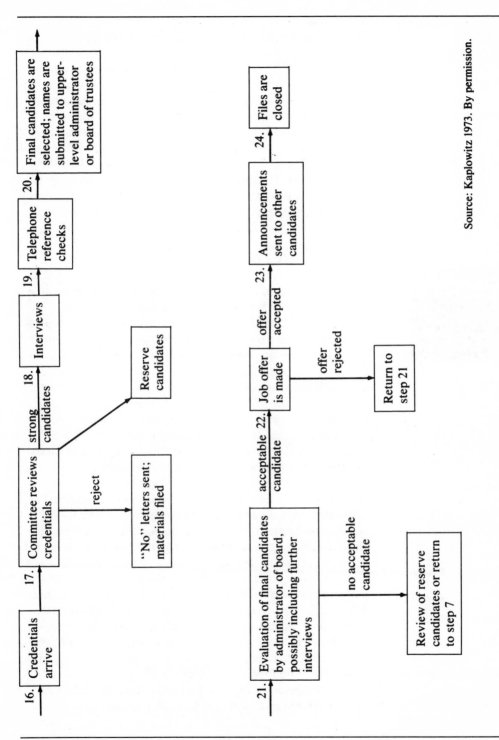

Source: Kaplowitz 1973. By permission.

tively, that task can be assigned to the search committee as one of its first tasks.

Basic organizational tasks include the selection (appointment and/or selection) of the members of the committee and the person to chair the committee; the charge to the committee; development of a timetable, secretarial support, office space, and meeting schedule; preparation of a job description; deciding where and how the job will be posted and advertised; doing the actual posting. Four key issues that arise during this phase are: the composition of the committee; communicating with candidates; confidentiality versus openness; whether a consultant will be employed to assist in the search.

Composition of the Committee

The chief executive officer of a campus or system normally is appointed by the board of trustees. Therefore, the search process is established by the board. In some few instances, the board will establish a trustee committee plus constituency advisory screening committees. The problem with more than one committee is that the advisory committee can "usurp the function of the selection committee . . . by concluding that only one candidate is suitable" (Nason 1980, p. 15). The potential political fallout when a faculty committee or an alumni committee develops a favorite candidate is obvious. In the more usual procedure, with one committee composed both of trustees and representatives of other constituencies, sensitivity is needed to address the numbers of slots to be allowed for each constituency, as well as whether that constituency will elect its members, nominate several candidates from whom the board will select, or whether the board will appoint the members. Respective campus norms generally determine the mode of selection of committee members.

A survey of presidential search committees found 17–18 members on search committees in public institutions, and 10–11 members in private institutions (McLaughlin 1983, AII). Forty-eight out of 52 committees reported that faculty members were included on the committee, and 43 out of 52 included students. In public institutions, the majority of search committees had fewer than half trustees; in private institutions, 50 percent had fewer than half trustees, and 50 percent included at least half trustees.

In many cases, the dynamics of a search committee would make rather special and very positive case studies for a course on the small-group process. Given an opportunity to work together, people selected from various constituencies, who initially approach their common concern from some very different perspectives, can and do develop a very positive sense of unity of purpose. In the good cases, while retaining their respective perspectives, committee members leave partisan loyalties behind in a collective search for the person who will provide the best leadership. In a study of 31 searches conducted for deans, for example, it was reported that the committee members, who were primarily faculty, with some students and a few members of central administration, acted as trustees for the university community as a whole and not as a group of delegates for separate factions (Lutz 1979).

On the other hand, searches can go sour—and they can create battles with lasting and painful repercussions. Kiersh reports on presidential searches on three campuses that "had to cope with heavy pressures, both internal and external, and with fears that threatened to tear the institutions apart" (1979, p. 34):

- Brooklyn College, where there was division between a board committee and a faculty committee; a board member is quoted as having said, "The board at times has felt ganged up on by the faculty committee" (p. 31).
- The University of Massachusetts, where several board members, angry at the governor whom they believed had forced the previous president out of office, "struck back at the governor by sabotaging any candidate who seemed to carry his blessing" (p. 32).
- Amherst College, where the faculty voted to boycott the search after the board of trustees' chairman announced the creation of a search committee "which would include six trustees plus four non-voting faculty representatives and four non-voting students" (p. 34). Additionally, people believed that in a school coeducational only for two years, by indicating that preference would be given to alumni, the chairman "was actually saying that only male candidates would be considered" (p. 34).

In 1981, the American Association of University Professors (AAUP) updated its 1966 statement, "Faculty Participation in the Selection . . . of Administrators." While recognizing that "the legal power of appointment rests" with the board, the AAUP "emphasizes the primary role of faculty and board in the search for a president" (p. 323). With respect to other administrative appointments, the AAUP expects a faculty role that "should reflect the extent of legitimate faculty interest in the position" (p. 324). But there can be significant differences on the extent of that "legitimate faculty interest." Further, while recognizing that the president makes the final choice for administrative appointments, the AAUP asserts, "sound academic practice dictates that the president not choose a person over the reasoned opposition of the faculty" (p. 324).

An analogy can be drawn between campuses and hospitals. In each case, highly qualified doctors (of medicine or of philosophy) have hired administrators, and delegated to them those management duties which the doctors prefer not to handle themselves. Responsibilities and power gradually have accrued to these administrators, and the administrators now make a majority of the operating decisions about what will happen in their respective institutions. Good hospital and campus administrators know, however, that should their respective groups of doctors ever unite around any particular issue, the power to determine what will happen often may rest with the doctors.

On campus, when the powers of the boards of trustees and the powers of the faculty collide, the board has legal sway, and boards can (and sometimes do) appoint presidents over the objections of the faculty. However, as it is clear that the faculty does have great power to impact the institution in many key ways, head-on power clashes generally are avoided if possible by astute players. Further, in public institutions, the political concerns of both the legislative and executive branches of state governments can be additional sources of vectors of power. Given this range of powerful forces that can be brought to bear around the selection of leadership on any campus, the argument for carefully building a constituency-inclusive committee appears compelling.

Communicating with Candidates

> *A college in New England advertised in September with*
> *an October reply deadline. After a "thank you for your*
> *interest, we'll be back in touch" letter, final candidates*
> *heard nothing until the following March. Many were no*
> *longer interested. A surprising number of candidates*
> *never heard anything after being told "we'll be back in*
> *touch." Even candidates who have been interviewed are*
> *occasionally never notified that someone else has been*
> *chosen* (Kaffer 1981, p. 16).

It is important to establish, at the start, a clear, consistent,
courteous, and timely pattern of comunication with candidates. And, unless specifically requested otherwise by a
candidate, search-related correspondence is *never* sent to a
candidate's business address, even if marked "personal
and confidential."

Careful and detailed recordkeeping is necessary, both for
the efficiency of the search committee and to provide materials in case questions (legal or other) are raised about the
process. A summary log recording all applications and the
actions regarding those applicants is suggested. Additionally

> *For each candidate there should be a file containing the*
> *initial application, additional application materials, writ-*
> *ten recommendations, records of telephone calls made,*
> *notes of telephone conversations, decisions made by the*
> *search committee at each stage of the search, interview*
> *records, and copies of all correspondence between the*
> *institution and the applicant/candidates* (Higgins and
> Hollander 1987, pp. 13–14).

Confidentiality versus Openness
Theoreticians and consultants alike emphasize the importance of confidentiality in a search process. This significance of confidentiality and the impact of openness as
required by sunshine laws in some states are discussed in a
subsequent chapter.

Consultants
The use of consultants in the search process in higher education has increased dramatically within the past 10 years. Many factors affect the decision on whether a consultant should be employed to assist in a given search. The role of consultants in educational searches is discussed later.

The Pool of Candidates
Some candidates indicate an interest in a vacant position themselves in response to postings; others are nominated for a position by various friends of the institution and/or as a result of the active seeking of appropriate candidates through various interpersonal networks.

The once controlling "old boys" network was properly vilified because of its limited membership. The concept of reaching out to people who might be able to identify good candidates for a vacancy continues to be valued, although the parts of speech have sometimes changed (from networks to "networking.") As part of the process of evolution, "new girls" networks appeared (Stent 1978); similarly, there are networks of members of various minority groups. One particularly helpful source cited for identifying qualified female candidates for upper-level administrative jobs on campus is the Office of Women in Higher Education at the American Council on Education, which is coordinated by Donna Shavlik and Judith G. Touchton (McMillen 1986b). The Office of Minority Concerns at the council, under Reginald Wilson, can be helpful similarly. The networks of people who are asked by competent searchers to identify potential candidates generally include affirmatively active elements today with a much broader range of contacts than was ever offered by the old "old boys" network.

A key rationale for posting a position is the desire to be sure that the widest possible pool of qualified candidates can be reached, including those not within the view of those who may be asked for nominations as part of networking. Places to post available positions:

- In the United States, the single best location for posting administrative positions generally is acknowledged to be in *The Chronicle of Higher Education.*

- The "Sunday Education Section" of *The New York Times,* and, for financial positions, *The Wall Street Journal,* also are common posting points.
- Most colleges advertise vacant positions in their largest regional newspapers and in local area papers as well.
- Professional journals and newsletters geared to administrative specialites—to business officers, student personnel administrators, etc.,—often carry notices of vacancies. The Association for Continuing Higher Education and the National University Continuing Education Association, for example, each publish newsletters 10 times a year ("Five Minutes with ACHE" and "NUCEA News") which include job postings for continuing education administrators. "Personnelite," published by the College and University Personnel Association, indicates vacancies for university personnel officers.
- Internationally, such publications as the "Times Higher Education Supplement" (London) and the "Bulletin" of the International Association of Universities (France) are used (Kaplowitz 1977; Nason 1980).

Several publications have emerged for the specific purpose of advertising positions to various minority communities. Affirmative action officers and consultants who have used these publications report that the ads, which tend to be expensive, simply don't produce responses. They believe that administrators in higher education—of all ethnic and racial backgrounds—who are actively looking for positions read the *Chronicle* postings and their respective professional journals/newsletters; that the other ways to recruit candidates—through broad networks and widely sought nominations—provide the balance of affirmatively sought out candidates.

Two issues are enmeshed in this entire discussion—*affirmative action* and the *process of actively seeking candidates.* A later chapter reviews current issues and concerns in the area of affirmative action.

Actively and aggressively seeking good candidates is vital if a search is to include the best possible candidate pool. "There was a time when presidents . . . were expected to receive 'a call' to a new post." But, applying

Actively and aggressively seeking good candidates is vital if a search is to include the best possible candidate pool.

for positions no longer is considered improper, and "community colleges in our survey relied heavily on public notices" (Nason 1980, p. 37). However, many of the potentially best candidates either are not actively seeking positions, or they at least publicly feel unable to declare themselves candidates for a new position because of the constraints of their current situations. The importance of actively and sometimes persistently seeking candidates is emphasized here: recruitment—including postings in all appropriate journals—supported by aggressive networking by members of the search committee to secure nominations of candidates who might not themselves apply, followed sometimes by the necessity of educating prospective candidates to the value of the position in order to secure their interest.

Pursuing candidates too aggressively, on the other hand, can infringe on the life of reluctant or non-candidates in harmful ways. During a search in Florida, a person whom the search committee wanted to recruit specifically had indicated his unwillingness to serve as a candidate; nevertheless, his name was retained on a roster by the committee. Under Florida's sunshine laws, the list of people being reviewed by the committee, including this non-candidate's name, was published in the newspapers, with negative political fallout for him on his home campus (McLaughlin and Riesman 1986). Some of the related issues for candidates are discussed in the chapters on consultants and on confidentiality.

Finally, to avoid discouraging qualified candidates, committees are advised to advertise only for resumes in an initial posting, and to wait to request references until after at least a first major screening has taken place. This recommendation is made both because, in many cases, a qualified potential candidate for a senior-level position may be ". . . wary of letting potential referees know that he/she is considering a change in position" (Higgins and Hollander 1987, p. 31); and to avoid unnecessarily burdening "the committee, the candidates, those serving as candidates' references, and placement offices" (Kaplowitz 1973, p. 17.)

Screening and Interviewing the Top Candidate(s)
If the skills and attributes needed for a particular position have been properly identified, search committees generally

are able to reduce fairly quickly the number of candidates to a small group. In most searches, reference checking begins at this point; in some cases, where the interest of particular candidates is being negotiated, the initial nominations included sufficient reference information to preclude the need for further checking until very close to the end of the process. A subsequent chapter provides a detailed discussion of securing and interpreting references.

Once a group of primary candidates is identified, the most common process is to invite each candidate to the campus for interviews and a visit. The notion of having 15 candidates parade through the campus in a three-day marathon, with each having 60 to 90 minutes of the committee's time, generally is a waste of the committee's and the candidates' time. Part of the committee's responsibility is to screen more thoroughly, and reduce visitors to between three and five or six candidates.

The best candidates normally want some opportunity to meet people on the campus and to get a sense of the larger community. Visits, which include exposure to various elements on campus, are the norm in most searches other than at the presidential level. One or more meetings with faculty groups, with various administrative officers, and sometimes with students generally are arranged.

In presidential searches, patterns vary widely. In some cases, particularly where confidentiality may be a particular concern, presidential candidates may meet with search and/or trustee committees at airport hotels removed some distance from both the campus and the candidate's home. Toward the other end of the spectrum, some interviews/ visits involve extensive on-campus exposure in what can become a spectacle. "In its most elaborate form, it will be a two- or three-day ordeal . . . like a beauty contest" (Porter 1983, p. 45); it also has been suggested that "the parade of more than one candidate across the campus invites a local popularity contest" and that "the vast majority of candidates, however, would not dream of accepting without knowing something about the institution at first hand" (Nason 1980, p. 63).

Some presidential search consultants now recommend that, where appropriate in terms of the candidates and the campus environment, the search committee should identify one final candidate who then is invited to visit the campus.

Concerns in that situation emerge from a sense that the campus constituencies may feel they've been presented with a "fait accompli" when they expected to have input regarding final candidates. The possible effect may be that the new president will arrive on campus with constituencies that do not feel invested in her or his success. On the other hand, it has been suggested that:

  a. *an effective committee will most likely produce a highly acceptable candidate;*
  b. *because most people on campus feel it important to be viewed favorably by the new president even if they were not part of the final screening, they very quickly will seek to move toward a positive working relationship with their new leader.*

All candidates invited to the campus usually will have the technical qualifications and abilities needed to handle the position. Visits and interviews tend to serve three purposes: to allow for in-depth interviews which might help make some fine distinctions among well-qualified candidates; to assess the "chemistry" or the "fit" between each candidate and the campus community; to sell that position to the candidate. Some suggest, however, that "the vaunted 'chemistry' between a candidate and the board is too highly valued over the record of experience" (Porter 1983, p. 46).

As each phase of the search is carried out, it is important particularly to remember that, in selecting campus leadership for the years to come, search committees are not possessed of magical screening devices, such as swords implanted in stones; likewise, candidates are not mythical heroes with divine guidance, wisdom, or protection. Each and all are merely mortals, trying to do their respective best in a challenging situation:

It is, I believe, insufficiently recognized how vulnerable [candidates] are to the process—or how sensitive should be the process—that focuses so strongly on them" (Porter 1983, p. 43).

FACULTY RECRUITMENT

In Hixson's cartoon, a department head is seen enthusiastically talking to a candidate for a faculty position:

I'm happy to say we can offer you a temporary assistant professorship. Except for salary, benefits, course load, research equipment, and access to tenure, it'll be just like a regular faculty position" (1985, p. 33).

The increased use of temporary and of part-time faculty members is, perhaps, one of three key topics in faculty recruitment in higher education today. The others include effective sources for recruiting faculty members and salary discrepancies.

Sources for Recruiting Faculty Members

Burke (1986) recently completed a study of faculty recruitment at research universities. After referencing 1950s and 1960s reports, which reflected closed, preferential, and nepotistic themes in the selection of new faculty at that time, she notes that:

A change has occurred. . . . Junior faculty recruitment in the 1980s begins with advertising; the search is public knowledge, and there is little apparent evidence that the apparent openness of the process is deceptive. . . . The value of open advertising is confirmed by the fact that of the 52 assistant professors interviewed, 28 had obtained their positions by responding to advertisements in professional journals (Burke 1986, pp. 7–8).

Others in the group cited notices "posted on bulletin boards . . . at institutions granting the Ph.D in that particular discipline" (Burke 1986, p. 8). "More than two-thirds of the departments typically attracted more than 50 applications for an assistant professor opening, and a healthy proportion attracted more than a hundred" (p. 11).

Several approaches are available for reaching and identifying prospective faculty members; an effective recruitment program will probably make use of an appropriate mix of most or all of them at appropriate times. These approaches include:

- *Individual identification.* For senior–level appointments, faculty members within the departments will be able to identify, by name and location, the key people in their respective fields. The recruitment of senior-level personnel (sometimes the current or emerging "superstars" of higher education) is clearly an active, aggressive process involving extensive selling; the primary actors usually are key faculty members working with the help of a dean or president.

- *Posting in the professional journal of the discipline.* These journals are perhaps the primary source for serious academics who may be willing to consider a move to another campus under the proper conditions. Proper conditions may range from good weather at the new campus to cloudy academic or socio-political weather at the existing site. Those completing doctoral programs tend to be frequent journal readers—or, at least, frequent readers of journal ads.
- *Posting in the Chronicle of Higher Education.* This is considered a good source, though perhaps second best when time allows the luxury of using the professional journal. While anticipated vacancies can be posted in journals, the lead time required for such postings sometimes can be a minimum of three months, and departments that become aware of faculty vacancies in March, April, or May (much less in July) often are unwilling to wait for the professional journals.
- *Posting at professional meetings.* Having potential employers and prospective candidates from all over the country in one place at one time can provide a very valuable opportunity for interviewing for positions about which there has been previous correspondence, as well as for initial postings and contacts. The mid-winter meeting of the Modern Language Association and the late summer meeting of the American Psychological Association are but two of many widely attended annual meetings. Poorly handled, of course, there can be a "meat market" atmosphere at a professional meeting that many find distasteful.
- *Posting at graduate schools.* Notices mailed to the various heads of departments and programs in the disciplines can be a good source of candidates.
- *Posting in the international arena.* Such agencies as the Association of Commonwealth Universities, the Colombo Plan, the African American Institute, the

Ford and Rockefeller foundations, and the World
Bank can be of help in recruitment.
- *Networking*. Direct contact with such people as graduate school department heads, editors, and others who
might know of emerging talent can generate good candidates. The key issue, as always, is the breadth and
depth of the networks established:

*One enterprising department chairman, needing to
choose three faculty members for a newly reorganized
history department . . . spent his summer reading manuscripts under consideration for publication . . . [He] was
able to identify and recruit three recent doctoral recipients, each of whom had a first book published within six
months after joining the new institution. Departmental
prestige was rapidly established* (Kaplowitz 1977, p. 3459).

Salary Issues: Market and Equity
Three issues that affect faculty salaries intersect and over-
lap in a tangled skein: the legal issue of comparable worth,
the impact of the non-academic marketplace, and concepts
of fairness on campus. Some of the entangling factors
include:

- The concept of fairness on a given campus, that
"professionals in widely different disciplines of the
same rank and experience . . . (should be) . . . paid
identically" (Bergmann 1985, p. 10).
- On some campuses, faculty members in such allied
health fields as occupational and physical therapy who
hold (or may be at work on) master's degrees may be
hired at the rank of assistant professor, while the doc-
torate may be required for that rank in the humanities.
- Some colleges within large universities work hard to
have salaries equalized by rank within the respective
colleges; however, wide disparities are found among
the various colleges of that university.
- A belief that "sex bias is probably implicated in many
salary differentials between academic departments"
(Bergmann 1985, p. 8).

- An assertion that "income disparities resulting from departmental differences are small in comparison with those resulting from the tendency for women to be concentrated in the lower academic ranks and in part-time, non-tenure-track positions" (Sherman 1985, p. 64).
- "A widening gap between salaries in academe and in the private sector," complicated by the cycle in which "private-sector demand for people with training in engineering, computer sciences, and business expanded more rapidly than the demand for all private sector personnel as a whole and thus accentuated the demand for faculty members" (Hansen 1985, p. 6).

Whatever the factors, and however much the use of market factors in determining faculty salaries may be "one of the most controversial practices in American higher education today" (Sojka 1985, p. 11), the reality of salaries in the latter half of the 1980s, as reflected by numerous surveys, is that:

> *At both private and public institutions of higher educa-tion, faculty members in fields where they are in high demand are commanding higher than average salaries this year, with accounting, business, and engineering topping the lists* (Evangelauf 1986, p. 25).

Temporary and Part-time Faculty Members
One major result of the "scarce resources and environmen-tal uncertainty" under which colleges and universities have been operating for the last decade "has been almost frantic attempts to experiment with different modes of academic staffing" (Mortimer, Bagshaw, and Masland 1985, p. 29). Summarizing their report, these authors note that fixed term and rolling contracts, non-tenure track appointments, and part-time faculty are three of the strategies at the point of hire that can help to increase needed institutional flexi-bility (1985, p. 30). The issues and impact of temporary faculty members, and of part-time faculty members (reported variously at 25 to 33 percent of all instructional personnel, and as more than half of all community college instructors), are discussed by a number of authors includ-ing Gappa (1984), Leslie, Kellams, and Gunne

(1982), Parsons (1980), and Townsend (1986). With respect to part-time faculty:

Our attempt to find norms was seriously frustrated. Our conclusion was that use of part-time faculty is a highly localized phenomenon, that disaggregation, rather than generalization, is essential to its understanding (Leslie, Kellams, and Gunne 1982, p. vi).

The qualifications for and use of part-time faculty varies from campus to campus and from discipline to discipline. For example, accounting faculties may prefer to have all basic-level courses taught by full-time faculty members, with expert part-time faculty members brought in to teach tax accounting; mathematics faculties may utilize the part-time faculty members in basic math courses, while the more esoteric theory of numbers and non-euclidian geometry courses are taught by the full-timers.

Part-time faculty members are recruited predominantly from the local community of the college. Effective and affirmatively active recruitment techniques include the development and maintenance of an active file of potential faculty members before the need for filling particular positions emerges. Continuing education deans and directors, who often have multiple lines into their communities, can be good sources of leads for potential part-time faculty. Also, some campuses, particularly those in or near urban areas, will run ads periodically, indicating clearly that they are seeking people interested in having their papers on file for prospective part-time openings.

Along with broad posting and appropriate salary offers, the quest for the best faculty members—the heart of the academic enterprise—can be assisted by a careful use of references, by effective interviewing, and by taking appropriately affirmative action.

THE USE OF CONSULTANTS

A major shift in the past 15 years has been the increased use of outside consultants in the search for campus administrators. Professional associations, non-profit agencies, major corporate search firms, and several dozen independent consultants have become involved in helping campuses with some or all phases of the search and selection process.

It is clear that an increasing number of institutions, from small church-related colleges to large public universities, from community colleges to prestigious liberal arts institutions, are finding it worthwhile to employ consultants in searches for college and university presidents (Riesman and McLaughlin 1984, p. 14).

Increased acceptance of the use of outside consultants on campuses probably can be traced to a confluence of several factors: "the growing recognition that recruiting suitable candidates for a position exposed to unusual stress may be difficult," (Riesman and McLaughlin 1984, p. 14); concerns for proper and legal affirmative action procedures and outreach; the broad acceptance of the practice in the corporate sector, brought to the campus both by board members and by increasingly visible business school faculty members; and by increasing numbers of successful campus experiences with consultants.

Who is providing the consulting services? What services do they provide and how can campuses make the best use of those services? And, what are the caveats and concerns in using consultants in a search?

Providers of Consulting Services

The Presidential Search Consultation Service (PSCS) is a not-for-profit consulting group jointly sponsored by the Association of American Colleges and the Association of Governing Boards of Universities and Colleges. The PSCS was created in 1976, with initial foundation funding, under the auspices of the AAC; in 1979, the AGB became a cosponsor. (Stead 1985, pp. 19–20). The PSCS is currently under the direction of Ronald Stead, with assistance from Bruce Alton; Frederic Ness, the previous director, continues to assist in searches, along with several other associates. The PSCS, which may be the most visible search con-

A major shift in the past 15 years has been the increased use of outside consultants in the search for campus administrators.

sultation group in higher education, assists in searches for chief executive officers, i.e., college and university campus and system presidents and chancellors.

Many other consultants also offer assistance. The Association of Community College Trustees has a search service. The non-profit Academy for Educational Development has a search division. One of the many private groups that provide consulting services is the Higher Education Administrative Search group, based in Denver, which tends to focus more at the vice-presidential level. Thompson and Pendel Associates, in Arlington, Va., a group which specializes in consulting about development to non-profit organizations, undertakes searches for institutional advancement officers. Joseph Kauffman, a well-published theoretician and practitioner, consults particularly in large state university system searches at the presidential and vice-presidential levels. Additionally, major corporate sector executive search firms (Korn-Ferry, Heidrick and Struggles, etc.) have established divisions that focus on presidential and other searches in the not-for-profit sector. (The particular groups and individuals listed are cited only as examples; more than 1,200 firms conduct executive searches in the United States [Zippo 1980, p. 47]. This listing does not, of course, constitute an endorsement of any person or group).

Another group that is sometimes listed in the context of consultants/search firms, but which does not do on-site consulting, is the Higher Education Administration Referral Service (HEARS), under the general sponsorship of the National Association of College and University Business Officers, plus 13 other cosponsor organizations. HEARS maintains an up-to-date data bank of close to 100 prospective candidates in each of about 70 different campus job categories. They will provide the resumes of prospective candidates to institutions subscribing to that service. Candidates can register to be in that data bank for a relatively small fee; a "confidential" registration is possible also. HEARS screens and selects candidates on the basis of listed qualifications for the particular vacancy; HEARS does not provide reference checking or other services beyond that point—perhaps placing HEARS someplace between simple posting and intensive personalized networking as a recruitment aid.

When considering a consultant, it is important to determine who within the consulting firm will be doing the work. In some cases, the person who makes the proposal either will conduct or will be a major part in conducting the search; sometimes the sourcing and preliminary screening of candidates is conducted by an associate, and the senior person is involved only in final screenings; in some cases, the person who sells the service is unrelated to the person who will provide it. It seems important to know and be comfortable with the people who will actually be doing the work.

For the campus which considers seeking the help of a consultant or consulting firm, it is important to remember the respective roles and relationships. The campus is the employer; the consultant is a hired adviser. The style, approach, and methods of the consultant must match or at least be acceptable within the climate of the individual campus client. Any consultant selected should reflect a clear sensitivity to and understanding of the respective roles, and of the particular campus climate. Consultants can have a significant impact on the long-term growth and development of colleges they assist. Good consultants have enough humility to recognize their own limitations and biases as well as their power to make positive contributions.

How to Make the Most of the Services Available
In addition to general help in structuring the search, consultants can offer special assistance in four major ways: securing good candidates who might not otherwise be available; maintaining confidentiality; checking references; moving the search along swiftly.

> *Whenever possible, the decision to employ a search consultant should be made . . . at the very outset of a search so that the consultant can guide the organization of the search process.* (Riesman and McLaughlin 1984, p. 14).

Some of the difficulties that can emerge when a search is launched without adequate preparation can include a cumbersome search committee structure, an inappropriate chairperson of the search, creation of a committee without

prior consultation with constituent groups, and lack of a clear charge to the committee (Stead 1985, p. 2).

Search consultants normally work directly with search committees on the campus. A consultant may be asked to locate, screen, and recommend independently one or several candidates; that is most likely to occur when a non-academic presidential staff vacancy, as in finance or institutional advancement, is being filled.

Search consultants can help the campus organize for a search. They can instruct in the importance of, and help structure the search for, confidentiality; assist in the identification and recruitment of candidates who might not respond to open postings; help in the screening of candidates; assist in structuring interviews; conduct reference checks; help in negotiations of contracts when a candidate is selected—which may include educating campuses about the current market salary figures for candidates under consideration. Riesman and McLaughlin (1984) provide a detailed discussion of the various ways in which consultants can help in a presidential search. These authors currently are at work on a book on the presidential search process; it will include a discussion of consultants in the process, as well as several case studies of presidential searches. (Publication is scheduled tentatively for 1987.)

A key element that appears to contribute significantly to their effectiveness is the network of contacts that search consultants have established. Many consultants in higher education searches are, or were, on college campuses in leadership positions and were generally widely involved with colleagues in professional associations during those years. Out of these involvements have come the affiliations that can provide two of the most important services of all—identification of qualified candidates and discreet in-depth reference checks.

In the discussion of confidentiality and openness in searches, the unwillingness of many potentially good candidates to be publically identified as candidates is noted. The informal network is replete with stories of otherwise interested candidates who have withdrawn from candidacy when their names became public. The effective search consultant will have both the concern for discretion and the professional network that will normally lead to more in-depth information on candidates without public disclosure of their candidacy. It is noted, however, that:

> *. . . most consultants will refuse to enter searches at a time when some search committees believe they could be especially useful: namely, when it comes to checking the references and exploring all possible information concerning finalists. As one search consultant explained, if the person chosen after this final checking turns out well, no one will remember who the search consultant was; if the person chosen turns out badly, everyone will blame the search consultant who came in at the end of the procedure. The search consultant is not so likely to be blamed if she or he has been operating with the search committee all along* (Riesman and McLaughlin 1984, p. 23).

Concerns and Caveats

A key concern related to the use of consultants in college searches is the feeling, cited frequently on campuses, that the constituencies on campus will be excluded from the process. Reporting on an Oberlin college search, Riesman and McLaughlin indicate that:

> *Far from regarding themselves as excluded by the employment of search consultants, many faculty concluded that they had more opportunity to influence the search . . . [for a new president] . . . than they anticipated* (1984, pp. 13–14).

A consultant who heads the non-profit division of a major executive search firm indicated that she has never encountered hostility in a faculty group, once the opportunity to meet with the faculty established both the legitimacy of the consultant and the opportunity of the faculty for input.

In some circles, executive recruiters are known as "headhunters." The key operative element in that frequently disliked label is the word "hunter." As has been noted, an active search for the hunter's "prey" (candidates, the "treasure" of the quest from the committee's point of view) has become an essential part of a search process. As active seekers of good talent, executive recruiters always are alert to the existence of such talent around them. Campuses may seek to protect themselves with an agreement from a search consultant that good people met on the campus during the consulting assignment will not be recruited for other positions on other campuses. In the corporate world, such agreements sometimes are negotiated, for at least a two-year span of time.

While many campus inhabitants may assume that there are large numbers of highly capable leaders who are anxious for the opportunity to come to their particular campuses in an administrative role, that is not always the case. Faculty members and others may need to be educated to the reality that the best candidates quite frequently are happy and successful in their current roles elsewhere, and are, in fact, sometimes people who normally read only the front half of the *Chronicle*. Riesman and McLaughlin suggest that:

> *Consultants are more likely both to know how to go about finding appropriate candidates and to have the requisite time and skills needed to persuade someone to consider a new position* (1984, p. 15).

Mottram even more emphatically states that:

> *The most compelling reason . . . for a college or university president to employ a search firm when looking for a key administrative officer is the opportunity to learn of outstanding candidates that might never surface in any other way* (1983, p. 40).

Search consultants privately express the opinion that, in the arena of disciplinary academic leadership—i.e., department heads—there is, and will continue to be, significantly more faculty resistance to the use of consultants; further, that such resistance often is valid. At times, there has been more heated discussion about deanships; consultants suggest that some faculty members view the deanship to be primarily an academic role, while others more accurately see the role as primarily administrative.

Two particular issues emerge for candidates when consultants do the reference checking. First, as such checks are invariably done orally, it may not be possible for candidates to refute a poor and perhaps inaccurate reference which may have been gathered by a consultant from an unidentified source.

Another possible hazard is that a consultant, having heard negative information about a candidate in one search, may blackball this candidate in other searches the consultant advises (Riesman and McLaughlin 1984, p. 21).

The validity of this concern was reinforced in a private conversation with a fairly active consultant; he indicated that in a recent search, out of 20 viable candidates who emerged after a committee's first screening, he already had some knowledge of 10 from previous search consultations.

The issue of fees and costs can be a concern to some campus constituencies, and is an item that recruiters rarely discuss in public or private, except in an actual contract proposal and negotiation. Fees range and vary: a flat rate may be negotiated; fees may be charged on an hourly rate or a per diem rate; and/or the fee may be based on the annual salary of the administrator being hired. For initial guidance, it may be helpful to know that, in the corporate sector, recruiters tend to charge the client company a fee that is someplace between 30 and 35 percent of the first year's salary of placed executives.

While some corporate placement fees for middle management positions are contingency-based (contingent on placement of a candidate), most executive search firms prefer to work on a fee basis, with installments paid as the search progresses; fixed rather than contingent fees appear to be the norm in academia. Fixed fees can serve the interests of both recruiter and client; a key problem with the contingent pricing method is that the recruiter may be "looking for a quick delivery, not the right person for the job" (Zippo 1980, p. 48). Expenses incurred by the consultant sometimes may be included in a total set fee, or a contract can be written which includes the consultant's fee plus expenses incurred. The PSCS, when funded by foundation grants in the earlier years, was significantly less expensive than other agencies and firms; that difference appears to have been somewhat narrowed.

Finally, a key note and caveat closes this review of consultants in the search process: "The client institution must retain the fundamental responsibility of choosing its president" (Hartley and Ness 1981, p. 37). An aspect of consulting that can be both ego-satisfying and frustrating for consultants is that they are paid for their opinions and for their advice. It always must remain clear within any consulting relationship, however, that the client campus or board retains both the authority and the responsibility to make the final decisions. "The authority to screen potential applicants can be subcontracted, but not the responsibility for ensuring a successful and fair selection process" (Rubenfeld and Crino 1981, p. 76).

CONFIDENTIALITY AND SUNSHINE LAWS

In search after search held "in the sunshine," I've watched colleges get refused by, or very quickly lose, most of the best candidates (search consultant, 1986).

Searches conducted "in the sunshine" are inextricably linked to issues of confidentiality. The loss of good candidates is identified in each of three key studies (Cleveland 1985; Kaplowitz 1978; McLaughlin 1983) as a major cost of what Cleveland labels a "trilemma" of clashing elements:

1. *The public's right to know . . .*
2. *The individual's right to privacy . . .*
3. *The public institutions's mandate to serve the public interest (1985, pp. 3–4).*

Searches conducted "in the sunshine" are inextricably linked to issues of confidentiality.

This chapter touches briefly on four aspects of confidentiality in the search process: the problems of disclosure or openness in a search; sunshine laws; maintaining confidentiality; and future considerations.

Openness and Disclosure

Two authors examined the issues relating to confidentiality in presidential searches and the negative effects, for candidates and campuses alike, of breaches in confidentiality during a search (McLaughlin 1983, 1985a, 1985b; McLaughlin and Riesman 1985, 1986; Riesman and McLaughlin 1984). Having come to the conclusion that "confidentiality is necessary to ensure the quality of the search committee discourse and the quality of the candidate pool" (McLaughlin 1985b, p. 24), they have included an exploration of sunshine laws as one among a number of ways in which confidentiality is lost in the search process in public institutions.

Confidentiality is important because "most major universities will not rely on fresh potential in a new president when a vacancy occurs. They will look for someone with a proven track record" (Ashworth 1982, p. 22). Such candidates, Ashworth and consultants alike suggest, are found through "piracy," and "the very nature" of the current positions of these treasures, these targets for piracy, tends to makes them unwilling to go public in considering another position, "for they do not want to risk eroding

Theodore Lownik Library
Illinois Benedictine College
Lisle, Illinois 60532

35

their effectiveness in their current positions'' (Ashworth 1982, p. 22).

On occasion, public knowledge of candidacy elsewhere might have a positive effect on an administrator's home campus. It would be difficult to imagine that the public knowledge that one had been on the list of the top 50 candidates in the most recent search to fill Harvard University's presidency (1970–71) could have had anything but salutary effects. Similarly, during the 1985–86 academic year, it was suggested that John Silber, president of Boston University, and James Halderman, president of the University of South Carolina, were each under consideration to fill the chair of secretary of education in Washington. Among many of their respective constituencies, this was interpreted as an affirmation of their prominence in the national higher education scene. In most cases, however, the result of disclosure of one's candidacy elsewhere is, at best, neutral. Quite often, it is deleterious. In one of the more extreme cases:

> *One university president allowed a search committee to put his name forward in an exploratory way. When news of his candidacy was leaked to the press, his campus and local community turned on him and his family, verbally abusing his children in school, dumping garbage on the front steps of his home, and publicly denouncing him as a traitor in the local newspapers. The situation became so ugly that he was forced to submit his resignation. When he was not the search's final choice, he found himself without a job* (McLaughlin 1985a, p. 206).

McLaughlin also notes that internal candidates have to contend with higher levels of scrutiny than do outside candidates. ''If the internal candidate is not chosen president, he or she has to deal with this loss publicly'' (1983, p. 5.10). Additionally, ''an internal candidate may have to confront an unknown future'' with a new boss arriving who may or may not be comfortable with an unsuccessful applicant still on campus. Confidentiality therefore can be of help to the internal candidate as well as to the candidate from another campus.

Sunshine Laws

*The mandate to serve the public interest is the basis,
implicity or explicitly, for most state open meeting laws
. . . As they have done before . . . the American people
through their elected representatives reasserted their
right to hold the reins of government in their own demo-
cratic hands* (Cleveland 1985, pp. 3, 5).

"Open Meeting or Sunshine Laws are statutes that
require that meetings of public bodies be held in public"
(Kaplowitz 1978, p. 2). Open meeting laws, intended to
assure that the general populace is able to remain informed
about the doings of government, appear to have their roots
in this country, rather than in our inherited common law,
and can be traced to the First Amendment of the U.S.
Constitution. The first state sunshine laws appeared in
Utah in 1898 and in Florida in 1905. Both the Joseph
McCarthy era of the 1950s and the Watergate era of the
early 1970s are cited as key factors in the relatively recent
and rapid expansion of this principle into legislation in all
50 states. (Cleveland 1985; Kaplowitz 1978).

Open meeting laws generally include definitions of what
constitutes a meeting and the list of the topics, if any, that
the state allows for consideration in executive sessions.
Topics allowed in executive sessions might include some
range of personnel matters; collective bargaining; consultation with legal counsel; security; and financial transactions
and plans, particularly relating to real property.

Cleveland's (1985) study provides a thorough update of
the 1978 (Kaplowitz) discussion about, and legislative summary of, sunshine legislation in the 50 states, along with an
important review of recent judicial findings and interpretations of the laws. Cleveland also defines and discusses the
"trilemma" of conflicting interests noted above.

*The clearest consensus . . . among observers in states
that both do and do not allow closed discussions of personnel matters is around the position that at least certain personnel items—notably recruitment and appointment of personnel—should be discussed in confidence*
(Kaplowitz 1978, p. 21).

Two key concerns surface repeatedly when personnel matters, by law, must be discussed in the open: the failure to recruit and keep good candidates, and the constraints on dialogue in the evaluation of the merits of candidates (or employees) being reviewed.

Three kinds of damage to the search process are cited:

- *. . . that most of those who would be the best candidates remove themselves from the pool, or never allow themselves to get into the pool . . .*
- *the process undergoes . . . distortions to discourse . . . leading to superficial discussions and letters of reference . . .*
- *an open process is also subject to manipulation for political ends . . .* (Cleveland 1985, p. 27–28).

As a specific illustration:

The search for a new president at the University of Florida provides dramatic evidence of the problems of conducting a presidential search in the sunshine . . . virtually none of the educational and political leaders were willing to be considered for the position. We know of no comparable search in which as many candidates declined even to allow their names to go forward (McLaughlin and Riesman 1986, p. 11).

"The effects of openness on the nature of discourse are the most far reaching of all" (Cleveland 1985, p. 21). Some of the suggested costs include a loss of candor, loss of the freedom of speech among decision makers, and a tendency toward simplistic and often trivialized discussions (p. 22).

Some consultants have suggested that very careful examinations of the constraints and wordings of some sunshine laws, in fact, do allow a search process to go quite far down the road toward its conclusion before openness is required. This position is challenged by other observers of current judicial and legislative decisions on the issue.

Maintaining Confidentiality
Clearly, in states with sunshine laws that do not make exceptions for personnel issues, confidentiality cannot be maintained. In other contexts, however, it is possible to

attempt to have confidential searches, either through to completion, or at least up to the point where final candidates are visiting the campus.

Several factors can contribute to leaks when a confidential search is under way, including;

1. The conditions under which the previous president departed, and/or problems with, or caused by, the departing president.
2. Major happenings on the campus that may be unrelated to the search—but then, as all presidents learn, nothing that happens on campus is unrelated to them.
3. A campus culture that expects openness.
4. The presence or absence of an aggressive press (public and/or student press).
5. The presence of internal candidates and politics emerging from that.
6. The commitment of individual search committee members to confidentiality, as well as to their other members of the committee, loyalties to constituencies, and their pleasure or displeasure with the directions of the board. (McLaughlin 1983, p. 5.4–5.9).

McLaughlin also makes a number of very helpful suggestions about how to reduce the likelihood of leaks in presidential searches, including initial and periodic discussions with the committee about confidentiality; dealing effectively with the press (perhaps one person only, and, from others, a consistent "no comment" may be best); involvement of consultants; using diversionary methods of conducting the business of the search such as maintaining the office and files off campus, and having all expenses paid privately until after the search is over (1983, 1985b).

From the perspective of confidentiality, the process of gathering references is one of the most vulnerable points in the process. Securing references effectively is discussed in a later chapter.

Looking Toward the Future
At a symposium held in May 1985, a group of discussants drawn from prominent newspapers, higher education associations, law firms, and elected and appointed public officials met to assess the Cleveland (1985) report. The partici-

pants emphasized the business that can be conducted effectively, and in the public interest, in the open. They also addressed the "most fundamental question involved in governance under open meeting laws . . . the determination of those topics that warrant . . . moving from public into executive session" (Kaplowitz 1978, p. 2).

The major thrust at this symposium was that "there is far more than most boards commonly assume that can be done in the open." Calling for guidelines to "help governing boards understand how much business they can conduct in public," participants agreed that the financial condition of the institution, evaluations of programs and of the institution as a whole, and personnel policies and procedure should be openly discussed, but that evaluations of individuals should be kept secret (Winkler 1985, p. 13).

It is hoped that the focus brought to bear on this issue, under Cleveland's direction, by the Hubert H. Humphrey Institute of Public Affairs will serve to encourage states to modify that singular aspect of open meeting laws where the impact is so evidently negative—the personnel arena—without vitiating the very important public interest aspects of these laws. In the meantime:

> *Support for the concept of open meetings is broadly based. . . . The advice suggested repeatedly is that it is crucial for all board members to know the provisions of the sunshine law under which they govern, and to be careful to work within those provisions* (Kaplowitz 1978, p. 23).

Or, in the words of one of the participants at the 1985 symposium, "Openness is here to stay . . . boards had better learn how to operate within the laws" (Winkler p. 13).

AFFIRMATIVE ACTION/EQUAL OPPORTUNITY

Under a headline that answers the question before asking it, Gelbspan and Kaufman asked:

> *Who has a better chance of getting a job in Boston: a black worker seeking membership in the bricklayers' or ironworkers' union—or a black professor seeking a faculty appointment at Harvard, the Massachusetts Institute of Technology, Boston University or Northeastern?* (1985, p. 1)

The headline's answer was "Blacks Faring Better In Trade Unions Than On Campuses." The authors further assert that, at least in the Boston area, "private universities . . . are steadily losing black faculty" (p. 18). A table titled "Full-time Black Faculty in Area Colleges and Universities" reflects declines in the percentages of black staff from 1979 to 1985: MIT, 1.8 percent to 1.0 percent; Northeastern University, 3.3 percent to 2.14 percent; Tufts University from 1.6 percent to 1.5 percent; and Wellesley College from 3.7 percent to 3 percent. In the Boston area, only the University of Massachusetts at Boston increased its percentage of black faculty members during the six-year period cited from 6.9 percent to 8.03 percent (p. 18).

These figures provide one indication of a multifaceted issue in higher education—facets that include statistical information, governmental and judicial shifts in direction, affirmative action policies and procedures for personnel searches and selection, and some critical long-term issues for higher education. The evolution of affirmative action legislation has been traced in detail elsewhere (e.g., VanderWaerdt 1982, pp. 77–79). This chapter will focus on issues in affirmative action in the later 1980s.

Statistical Update

In a field where much data is collected and yet little is widely available, some of the best data on percentages of females and minority group members in the administrations and faculties of two-year American colleges and universities come from two studies undertaken by Joseph Hankin, president of Westchester Community College. In presenting his findings, Hankin reported "both good news and bad news" (1984, 1985). Studying 86.6 percent of all U.S. public community colleges, Hankin (1985) found:

- *29.4 percent of the administrators were female.*
- *36.6 percent of the faculty members were female.*
- *13.4 percent of the administrators were members of minority groups.*
- *10.2 percent of the faculty members were members of minority groups.*
- *39.2 percent of the administrators were female and/or minority group members, an increase from 25.7 percent in 1975.*
- *42.8 percent of the faculty members were female and/or minority group members, an increase from 39.2 percent in 1975.*

Another study, on academic deans hired in colleges and universities with more than $1 million in federal research support, stated that "white females nearly doubled the rate at which they are filling academic dean positions (15.5 percent) compared to the rate at which they are vacating positions (8.2 percent)"; black males and females, however, "made no gains" in achieving academic deanships (Rodman and Dingerson 1986, p. 28). Hispanic participation in the administration of 106 California community colleges was found to be concentrated in fewer than 25 percent of the 70 college districts (Rivera 1983).

A study of women chief student-affairs officers reflected that they were younger somewhat than male chief student-affairs officers (average ages 37 vs. 44), that more than half of each group held comparable doctoral degrees, that women were more likely to be at smaller and at private colleges than men (56 percent of women in institutions with populations under 2,000), and that, while a larger percentage of the women held faculty rank, men with faculty rank were more likely to be at higher ranks (Evans and Kuh, 1983).

A non-statistical report on a comparative study on the attitudes of mid-level managers toward affirmative action and toward employment of women in the public sector in 1973 and in 1983 found that:

It is likely that these 1983 managers have internalized at least the symbolic message of equal opportunity . . . and the majority acknowledged their own responsibilities for implementation (251) . . . Gone are the overt jokes or

hostile comments about "women can't do that" (256)
. . . [and] that equal opportunity goals are being internalized but that a residue of traditional sex role expectations is retained by both managers and workers (Huckle
1983, p. 257).

While Wilson (1985) noted that "the number of black
students in higher education doubled from 600,000 to 1.2
million between 1960 and 1980" (p. 20), he also found that
"black participation in higher education peaked in the late
1970s and has declined gradually during the 1980s" (p. 21).
Other statistics reflecting declines in more recent years
included a drop in the proportion of black New York State
youngsters who go to college, from 20.7 percent in 1975 to
19.4 percent in 1980, and of Hispanic students in that
period, from 20.4 percent to 16.1 percent; a drop in minority students receiving student aid of 12.4 percent in 1983–
84 from two years earlier (Hankin 1986). Further, black
participation rates in postgraduate education have declined
since the early 1970s with significant implications for future
staffing.

Further, black participation rates in postgraduate education have declined since the early 1970s with significant implications for futher staffing.

The Governmental and Judicial State of Affairs
When the Reagan administration took office in 1981, concerns were expressed that the enforcement of affirmative
action laws and policies would suffer. These concerns were
answered by the administration with statements that the
affirmative action offices would have no reductions in staff.
That response was received with some doubts. For example, the apocryphal "street talk" among human resource
personnel at New England high-tech government contrac-
tors was that, while there might be a promise of no reduc-
tion in staffing, the total annual travel budget for the gov-
enment's New England regional affirmative action office
was to be $11, which would clearly have some impact on
field enforcement.

A summary of the very positive progress made in the
United States with respect to equality of opportunity since
1941, attributed in large measure to governmentally required and court supported affirmative action, is followed by the statement that "the Reagan Administration . . .
has adopted (and appointed persons to carry out) a philosophy opposed to affirmative action" (Wilson 1985, p. 20).

For many, remedy for inequitable treatment has been found in federal executive agencies' enforcement of equal opportunity requirements, and in the courts. Numbers of our campuses operate within the terms of negotiated affirmative action plans and goals, recorded in court supervised settlements known as consent decrees. Affirmative action requirements have generally been reinforced by court decisions. An example is the ruling, based on findings by the federal district court, that the University of Rhode Island "was guilty of discriminating against female faculty members" (Watkins 1985, p. 23) by offering lower starting salaries and lower ranks; the approval of both the faculty union and the affirmative action officer at URI are now mandated before any candidates can be offered faculty positions. "Judge Selya criticized the university for what he called 'high-level' footdragging over affirmative action for more than a decade" (p. 24).

The Civil Rights Commission has concluded that "seven of the nine judges have now approved the most vigorous sort of affirmative action" (Wilson 1985, p. 20). Even decisions in the courts, however, can be clouded. William B. Reynolds, the United States Assistant Attorney General for Civil Rights, has been at the center of several controversies over the interpretations of Supreme Court rulings. A 1984 decision

> . . . was interpreted by Mr. Reynolds as barring any preferential treatment of minorities unless the individuals aided could prove that they had personally suffered discrimination . . . He used that interpretation to try to overturn dozens of consent decrees . . . six federal appeals courts have rejected his interpretation (Fields 1986b, p. 10).

Wygant v. Jackson Board of Education (Case No. 84-1340) was decided by the Supreme Court in May 1986. While striking down an affirmative action agreement that protected the jobs of minority schoolteachers during layoffs, a majority of the court

> . . . rejected a central tenet of the Administration's attack on affirmative action—its contention that the

Constitution bars any race-conscious preferences in
employment, except to aid proven victims of bias . . .
Justice Sandra D. O'Connor said in a concurring opin-
ion last week that she and her colleagues agreed that an
affirmative action plan "need not be limited to the reme-
dying of specific instances of identified discrimination"
. . . In the deciding opinion, Justice Lewis F. Powell,
Jr., indicated that hiring goals would be more accept-
able to the Court than preferential layoffs" (Fields
1986a, pp. 1, 15).

Interpretations of this decision have been mixed. Within 10
days, it was reported that Assistant Attorney General Reynolds, who has been conducting a campaign to rewrite
Executive Order 11246, said that the decision

. . . would require the Administration to repeal at least
part of an executive order that has been used to require
colleges, universities, and other employers with govern-
ment contracts to launch affirmative action programs to
hire and promote more women and members of minority
groups (Fields 1986b, p. 10).

Reynolds' interpretation "was immediately rejected by a
spokesman for the Labor Department, which enforces the
order" (p. 10).
On July 2, 1986, the Supreme Court spoke even more
definitively, with rulings that

. . . rejected the Reagan administration's reading of a
1984 Supreme Court decision, which it contended sup-
ported its view that affirmative action may be used only
in helping identified victims of past discrimination, not
members of disadvantaged groups generally (Shepard
1986, p. 1).

This clear statement came in a pair of 7–2 votes:

The Supreme Court, repudiating the central principle of
the Reagan administration's civil rights policies, yester-
day strongly endorsed the use of affirmative action,
including specific racial goals, to remedy past employ-
ment discrimination. The Court, for the first time, said

federal judges may set goals and timetables requiring
employers who have discriminated to hire or promote
specific numbers of minorities . . . The decisions were
among the clearest pronouncements on affirmative action
in the Court's history (Kamen and Marcus 1986, p. 1).

Policies and Procedures

"An effective affirmative action program is designed to
provide equal consideration for all applicants for faculty
and staff positions" (VanderWaerdt 1982, p. 4). "Affirmative action and equal opportunity provisions call for seeking the best possible person for a job, regardless of race,
sex, age, or other extraneous factors" (Kaplowitz 1973, p.
7). An institution "must go out and search all the avenues,
nooks, and crannies to find the best candidates . . . it must
never forget the meaning of the words 'affirmative
action' " (Hankin 1985, p. 14). In summary, it is necessary
to actively (affirmatively) seek out qualified candidates
from all arenas, and to be sure that each candidate is evalu-
ated for the position on the basis of her or his individual
qualifications and fit for the position in question.

Pursuant to Executive Order 11246, an Affirmative
Action plan must contain two basic ingredients—narra-
tive sections which describe the contractor's good faith
efforts to achieve affirmative action in employment, and
statistical analyses which analyze the contractor's prog-
ress and problem areas, including the setting of annual
goals to remedy identified deficiencies (Stewart, Stickler,
and Abcarian 1985, p. 1).

It is neither the focus nor the intent of this section to
detail the policies, procedures, and practices that contribute to an effective affirmative action office. Further, such
an attempt would be redundant, as that need has been
addressed very comprehensively by VanderWaerdt (1982).
While search-related notes from that work are cited in this
review, attention is referred to the text in its entirety for a
detailed yet non-technical introduction to effective and
equitable affirmative action on campus. The need for
involvement of the affirmative action officer in each phase
of the search process from its beginnings is clearly deline-

ated by VanderWaerdt (pp. 19–26); she specifically suggests that one role for the affirmative action director might be that of "the campus expert on hiring" (p. 20).

The affirmative action director needs to demonstrate a clear commitment both to the special interests represented by that office and to the overall welfare of the institution. That includes ensuring that candidates identified through affirmative action networks have the necessary qualifications for the particular post to be filled. Further, it requires that the affirmative action officer model and demonstrate the high professional standards we seek of all search participants. The affirmative action officer who leaks confidential information about the search, in an effort to force a search committee's hand, damages the credibility of all affirmative action efforts on that campus.

Well-designed and effectively administered affirmative action programs do work. The success of the University of Massachusetts at Boston in increasing the proportion of minority faculty members on campus can be ascribed to the strong commitment of the chancellor to ethnic diversity, which was manifested in 1979 through a formal organizational increase in the power of the (very effective) director of affirmative action (Reynolds 1986). Similarly, Hyer's (1985) case studies reported and illustrated successful programs that led to increases in the proportion of women faculty members on three very different types of campuses; the key factors found common to these successes were:

1. commitment and leadership from the top—presidents and/or provosts;
2. women speaking out in their own behalf and providing leadership and energy;
3. in two of the cases, government pressure for an affirmative action plan as an initial catalyst.

Critical Long-Term Issues
In order to hire qualified people, the qualified people have to be there in sufficient numbers to provide an adquate pool of candidates. In too many searches, one woman and/ or one minority group member ends up among the 6 or 10 or 15 final candidates identified. At least in part, that appears to be because, statistically, sufficient numbers of

qualified women and of qualified minority members are not yet available for us to be able to totally ignore sex or race. Action still needs to be affirmative in any given search to generate a pool of well-qualified candidates that includes women and minorities in reasonable numbers. And it appears that the pace at which the pool is developing is different for women and for minority members.

An affirmative action officer indicated that finding qualified women is less difficult than it used to be. She cited her own campus, which had been statistically "overutilized" in terms of women on the basis of the 1970 census, which then became "underutilized" on the basis of 1980 data, because of the significantly increased availability of women. Increasing numbers of women appear to be "in the pipeline." While the numbers of women on campuses are increasing, women still are significantly underrepresented in major college policy making positions, women administrators are paid less than male administrators, and the problems are especially severe for minority women. (Finlay and Crosson 1981).

On the other hand, observers have noted that in 1979 blacks represented only about 4 percent of all professional and doctoral degree recipients (Hankin 1985); and a "decline in new black Ph.Ds from 1,400 a year in 1979 to about 1,000 a year today" (Gelbspan and Kaufman 1985, p. 18). Additionally, the career directions selected by black candidates don't favor higher education:

> *"Fewer blacks than expected are emerging from the academic pipeline . . . (the equal opportunity officer) blamed the phenomenon on more lucrative opportunities in corporate and professional jobs and a decline in the demand for teachers"* (Gelbspan and Haufman 1985, p. 18).

These two trends were joined in a September 1986 front page *Chronicle* headline, "Women Flock to Graduate Schools in Record Numbers, but Fewer Blacks are Entering the Academic Pipeline" (McMillan and Heller 1986, p. 1). Statistics reflect a negative change of 19.2 percent in the numbers of blacks in graduate schools between 1976–77 and 1984–85, an actual decline of about 12,500 black students. Graduate school enrollment increased for Hispanics (by about 4,000, an increase of 20.4 percent) and for Asians (by about 10,000, an increase of 54.5 percent); 40,000 more women (+ 7.8 percent) also were enrolled, although

> Women's representation in mathematics and the sciences, however, remains spotty . . . women received just 9 percent of the 1,078 doctorates awarded in physics and astonomy in 1985. In mathematics, they earned 15 percent of the Ph.Ds and in chemistry, 20 percent . . . [And] women with science doctorates have a higher unemployment and underemployment rate than men (McMillan and Heller 1986, p. 25).

Perhaps the key long-term issue is the development of the potential of all students who might someday staff our colleges and universities. Gelbspan and Kaufman cite the recollections of one black scholar:

> Although he excelled as a student at Harvard, winning honors and voted head of a student academic council, he watched his professors invite white students to their homes to court them for their faculty potential. He never received such an invitation—despite his outstanding record (1985, p. 18).

Recognizing that "we must not expect monodimensional solutions to multidimensional problems," Hankin urges multifaceted approaches to attract and recruit minority faculty members, including "mentors and role models, networks and nurturing climates" (1985, p. 16). He encourages support for programs like New Jersey's Hispanic Leadership Program; societal attention to the intertwined issues of housing, employment, and education; involvement of female and minority alumni to help recruit prospective students if white males are the only available campus-based recruiters; devotion of time and attention to the retention of minority students moving toward the completion of the various academic end points; and the recruitment and development of minority administrators from among the faculty (1985, pp. 16–17).

Aside from the need to draw upon the talents of the best from all sectors of society, the need to have females and members of minority groups in leadership positions as one aspect of affirmative action has been noted frequently. The reason usually suggested is that it is important to provide role models for female and minority students and faculty members. Seeing female and minority leaders also is quite important for non-female and non-minority group members as well—particularly if so many of the stereotypes that bedeviled previous generations are to be absent from the minds of future generations.

VanderWaerdt lists steps for the chief campus officers to take to assist in short- and long-term efforts, including being informed; highlighting efforts in speeches; working with community leaders to engage their help in recruiting both faculty and students; supporting professional development programs on campus; and questioning hirings and promotions which do not contribute to goal achievement (1982, p. 8).

Women may have had different career patterns than men; if the career patterns of men are taken as the "norm," then the resumes of women may appear deviant to a search committee. Careful readings of the resumes of women, attention to job requirements rather than previous career paths, distinguishing between candidates who have held particular positions and those who have performed jobs well, and reading the research that candidates have done are suggested as ways of assuring that female candidacies do not fail unfairly (Bartlett and Barnes 1978).

Specific recent actions to help "convince minority group members that faculty careers will, in the future, be prestigious, rewarding, and available" (McMillen and Heller 1986, p. 26) include increased graduate and postdoctoral fellowships in Florida (the McKnight Foundation's Black Doctoral Fellowship Program); a joint Ford Foundation/National Research Council five-year minority doctoral fellowship program; similar legislatively funded programs in New Jersey, Michigan, and Connecticut. New Jersey's Minority Academic Careers Program is cited as a model because it forgives students one-quarter of their loan for each year they teach in the state after they receive their degree. The Big 10 plus the University of Chicago have sponsored fellowships since 1978 that help support minority students in graduate programs in the sciences. A new National Consortium for Educational Access ". . . intends to identify minority undergraduates at 26 historically black colleges and help support them through Ph.D programs at nine research universities'' (McMillen and Heller 1986, p. 26). Programs in California also are focusing on alerting talented minority undergraduate juniors and seniors to opportunities in graduate education.

Other recommendations and approaches to the development of women and minority group members include administrative training programs as a strategy for advancing in higher education administration (Kanter and Wheatley 1978); organizations, networks, and caucuses, along with internships and other training programs (Finlay and Crosson 1981; Stent 1978); vita banks of minority and women candidates, although these have met with mixed results at best (Heller 1985); increasing the number of women and minority group members on governing boards, providing such specifically tailored developmental activities as the appointment of women to budget and finance committees, and planned mentor relationships (Ernst 1982; Moore 1982); developing sponsorship among people who have political savvy and strength, and whose judgment and recommendations are trusted (Kauffman 1978).

DESIRED ADMINISTRATIVE ATTRIBUTES

The effect of the successful adventure of the hero is the unlocking and release again of the flow of life . . . this flow may be represented . . . dynamically as a streaming of energy (Campbell 1968, p. 40)

"Looking for 'God on a good day' " (Healy 1985, p. 45); seeking "the president as 'reasonable adventurer' " (Pray 1979, p. 22); trying to find "executives possessed of remarkable strengths . . . who know how to handle adversity" (McCall and Lombardo 1983, p. 26, 30); the quest, the search for the monomythical heroes, for leadership, for renewed vitality in the academic endeavor . . .

It is difficult to recruit, identify, and select the "right" leadership for a campus. Even with the increasing number of books and articles filled with good advice, and despite the best efforts of search committees, we frequently fail.

In a . . . study of 32 colleges that had selected new deans, only slightly more than half of the deans selected indicated they would accept the position again if given the choice. About the same percentage of more than a hundred responding search-screening committee members said they would select the same person as dean if they had the opportunity to choose again (Lutz 1979, p. 261).

Further, the "right" person at a given point in an institution's development no longer may be appropriate 6 or 10 years later. The "builder" president may be a very ego-strong, internally-directed person who is able to push, cajole, convince, and sometimes bully boards, faculties, and/or legislatures into supporting major campus facility and program expansions. That is a process, however, that can deplete political capital, and create what gradually can become a critical mass of enemies. Successful "builder" presidents quite often are forced eventually to leave their expanded campuses, to be succeeded by low key, other-directed, listening and stabilizing leadership, for a "consolidation" phase. Similarly, the need may be for an administrator who is a tough labor negotiator at one point in the development of a faculty union on campus, and for a conciliator at another. The "right" qualifications and attributes are often situational.

> *The "right" qualifications and attributes are often situational.*

To assist in the selection of effective leadership for the campus, this chapter reviews some of the current research on factors that contribute to effective leadership; it then examines some of the particular attributes and skills that seem to support the effective performance of presidents and of chief academic officers, and, more briefly, of other selected campus administrators.

Leadership

Presidential leadership, although not the only ingredient, has been found to be a crucially important factor in a study of successful colleges that are growing and that are striving for academic excellence. An orientation to people, vision, opportunity consciousness, visibility, and a practical approach are suggested as some of the key traits of effective campus leaders (Gilley, Fulmer, and Reithlingshoefer 1986). Numerous similar lists of the traits of effective leaders have been compiled. Attributes on these lists generally can be grouped in one of three ways: interpersonal abilities, personal attributes, and technical management skills. Two of the most helpful such compilations are those of McCall and Lombardo (1983) and Walker (1979).

Assessing 20 out of 41 executives who had successfully "arrived" against 21 who had their upward movement "derailed," McCall and Lombardo found that "the most frequent cause for derailment was insensitivity to other people" (1983, p. 28). Overall, they identified 10 categories of fatal flaws, eight were intra- or inter-personal, and two were technical.

> *Only two things . . . differentiated the successful from the derailed: total integrity, and understanding other people. (Integrity means) . . . I will do exactly what I say I will do when I say I will do it. (And) . . . if I change my mind, I will tell you well in advance so you will not be harmed by my actions* (McCall and Lombardo 1983, p. 30–31).

Walker (1979, p. 2–5) identifies the world views of less- and more-effective campus administrators, suggesting that the less effective administrators are "taken" with the status of their position, and preoccupied with its authority and privileges; react with threat, and a punitive sense of "going after" those who have come after them; view decisions individually rather than in a larger context of interactive problems; eventually view faculty members as perverse and students as naive and mischievous. Conversely, more effective administrators wear the status and privileges of office lightly, separating themselves from their office with egos that "are not bulky." They view the academic community as a group of legitimate constituencies with differing interests. Their administrative style is pragmatic; they view administration as a process, and events as being related. They also have a sense of self-confidence.

The Presidency

> *The choice of a new president or chancellor is the most important and far-reaching responsibility of any board* (Gale 1980, p. 4).

Studies have been validating the long held belief that presidents "make a difference" (Kerr 1984). This section gathers some of the findings and observations of both theoreticians and practitioners to suggest the qualities that might be desired when seeking new presidential leadership. These include:

- Being a *"reasonable adventurer"*—a president who listens well, gets staff viewpoints and help, yet makes decisions alone; who expects much of both self and staff; who is open in thought processes; who is a friend without being a buddy to associates; and who is time conscious, priority conscious, and goal oriented (Pray 1979).
- In a community college, *knowing the historical, social, and economic undercurrents* of the college; using the organizational structure to facilitate progress toward goals; communicating openly through formal and informal networks; identifying and avoiding ego traps; knowing and influencing positively the culture and values of the college (MacTavish 1984).
- In a secular private liberal arts college or university, the president needs to *"be qualified to serve* as the institution's philosophical, community, political, aca-

demic, and administrative leader'' (Freeman 1985, p. 29).

- All presidents need the *capacity for educational leadership;* a commitment to excellence; teaching and administrative experience; a capacity for sound organization; tact, diplomacy, patience, and a sense of humor; the gift of persuasion; broadness, tolerance, and a demonstrated concern for the betterment of society (Strider 1981).
- Instead of seeking God on a good day, Healy believes that "universities need *leaders who can think, dream, envision, and image the future*" (1985, p. 22); also, leaders who can be spokespersons and symbols; who, because the job is so very reactive, have an internal awareness of when the job is being done well; who have the knowledge of how to relax and take vacations.
- Fisher and Tack (in research to be published in 1987) suggest that the most effective college presidents are *risk takers* who rely on respect, believe less in close collegial relationships than typical presidents, work longer hours, make decisions more easily, and confide less in other presidents than do their counterparts at other institutions (McMillen 1986a).
- Presidents who have *increased institutional strength* make strong appointments; devote considerable time to the details of management; appear to have a highly developed intuition for finances; establish priorities for their own agendas and concentrate on those; value and trust their faculties but, at the same time, resist faculty incursions on management prerogatives; they know the fundamental nature of higher education and what things will not work (Mayhew 1979).

Fisher (1984) categorizes power as being charismatic, expert, coercive, legitimate, and/or reward-based. He suggests that charismatic leadership—which inspires trust and confidence with a combination of distance, style, and perceived self-confidence—is the primary key to effective leadership, and, when coupled with expert and legitimate power, to an effective presidency.

One study reflects some differences between professed perceptions of an ideal candidate and the focus on the interpersonal attributes in lists of effective presidential leadership. Findings were that 77.9 percent of faculty members in Oklahoma desire administrators who are higher in initiating structure than in the consideration dimension, 17.6 percent desire a higher consideration dimension, and 4.5 percent desire both characteristics equally (Ghaemmaghami, 1984).

Green carefully notes swings of the pendulum with respect to leadership styles. Further, she warns that, while "adversity often breeds the wish to find a savior—a heroic individual who can make the bold and difficult decisions" (1986 p. 18)—when a leader, acting under stress, has used power to move an institution singlehandedly:

> . . . damage will be done to long-term issues, to morale, and to the institutional value system. When the crisis has passed, the leader will inevitably have to pay attention to the frightened and demoralized faculty who were not fully part of the rapid change process . . . to ignore the traditions of faculty input and the need for self-determination threatens the ability of an institution to continue to plan, adapt, and move forward as a body . . . Faculties will find a way to sabotage academic decisions about which they were not consulted . . . Few can lead long without the consent of the governed (Green 1986, pp. 18–19).

Suggesting that "definitions of effective contemporary business management sound like classic descriptions of college presidents" (1986, p. 20), Green concludes that there is no single formula for successful presidential leadership; rather, that leadership is situational, and presidents need a personally authentic approach to leadership that is solidly grounded in their convictions.

In the (not-very-distant) past, the list of requirements for a president would have included an additional item: an able, available, and supportive spouse. In light of societal changes still unfolding, it appears sufficient to indicate that, while a supportive spouse is a nice thing to have in anyone's personal and professional life, she or he no longer is a part of the official presidential "deal," unless separately contracted with and hired. The gender and marital status of presidents are no longer assumed. Presidents may be male or female; if the presidents are married, their spouses may be professionals in their own arenas, parents of small children, and/or graduate students; and their roles may change as their own lives evolve. "Trustees might have to consider . . . that they can no longer pay the price of getting two persons for one salary in this changing society" (Thompson and Thompson 1983, p. 46). On a related subject, it is noted that some presidents have even begun to use the on-campus "president's house" as an entertainment area only, while living in privacy with their families off campus. A final commentary on the listing of qualifications for the presidency is Trachtenberg's observation:

> *I was quite struck by the fact that before I came to (this campus), the faculty seemed terribly concerned about my academic background and about my position on a variety of matters having to do with teaching, research, learning, and scholarship. After my inauguration, however, I was struck by how unpopular I could become by continuing to address these very issues* (1981, p. 8).

Chief Academic Officers—Deans, Et Al.

> *The title "dean of the faculty" . . . suggests . . . that the officer so designated is the focus of the relations between the faculty of a university and the corporate entity as represented by the president and the board . . . the dean of the faculty should be both the chief representative of the president to the faculty through the schools and departments and the recognized representative of the general faculty in the higher levels of university administration . . . His job is to be a leader in the educational functions of the university* (Brown 1977, p. 204).

Brown suggests some qualities that help the individual function effectively, including an ability and willingness to simplify bureaucratic practices, and spending much time on extended face-to-face interactions with senior officers, department heads, and faculty members.

Four factors found to be indicators which discriminate effectively between poor and outstanding academic deans are: intellectual efficiency; flexibility; knowledge about the position; and judgment (Skipper 1982).

The criteria which appear to have a bearing on a dean's likelihood to succeed were examined (Heald 1982). Criteria used by search committees looking for deans of education were gathered in two ways: first, by examining the job postings, and then by surveying the chairpersons of those search committees; then, the opinions of the deans selected as a result of those same searches were surveyed for the deans' collective sense of the factors that are important for their success on the job. Seven key factors appeared on both group's lists of their 10 most important criteria. Leadership skill and decision making skills were the two top factors on each list. The other five criteria common to both the committees' and deans' lists were: sensitivity to faculty needs, program development skills, faculty relations skills, communications skills, and a vision for education. Further, several inconsistencies between published criteria and those actually considered important were noted in Heald's study:

- *"Demonstrated scholarship"* was the most frequently cited criterion in published postings, yet search chairpersons ranked it as the 13th most important criterion for selection, and deans as 27th most important for performing the job. Similarly, research commitment, which was the third most often published criterion, was ranked as 19th and 25th by chairpersons and deans, respectively.
- *"Vision for education"* was included on only two lists of published criteria, yet it was ranked ninth in importance by the search committee chairpersons, and third in importance by the deans. "Faculty relations skills" was on the published list of only one institution, yet it was ranked seventh by search chairpersons and sixth by deans.
- *"Planning and evaluation skills"* were cited in only two of the position postings, yet they were ranked fifth in import by the deans; similarly, "health and vigor" was listed by only one institution, yet it was ranked as seventh most important by the deans (Heald 1982).

An earlier study (Reid and Rogers 1981) similarly examined the mechanics of the search process, the composition of search committees, the reasons for candidate selection, and the background data of successful candidates in 45 schools that hired provosts or vice presidents for academic affairs. Two key findings reported were that experience as a dean was more important than experience as a department chair for candidates in large institutions, while the reverse was true in small, private institutions; and that faculty members reached beyond their own limits in selecting leadership, e.g., selected candidates had more, and more prestigious, publications than did the faculty members selecting them.

In a study that examined both the managerial skills needed by deans and the various career paths to the deanship, out of eight categories of management skills listed, the two most important skills were identified as (1) program planning and implementation, and (2) using personnel effectively (Sagaria and Krotseng 1986). This study also found that two paths—faculty to chairperson to dean, and other-administrator to dean—developed necessary skills for the management aspects of the deanship better than did other paths to the deanship.

In a personalized review on his 11 years of service as dean of the faculty of arts and sciences at Harvard, Rosovsky (1987) reflected on the management skills needed for effective senior-level university administration. He included being able to

- *listen to constructive gossip;*
- *balance a number of special interests;*
- *deal with the press;*
- *ask for money ("an excellent way to test the free market") (p. 39);*
- *avoid confusing the privileges of representing one's institution with personal entitlement;*
- *take charge of 15,000 people and rather large budgets.*

In summary, Brown (1984) suggests that the leadership roles of chief academic officers include strategic planning, budgeting, an awareness of emerging technologies, faculty leadership, and faculty development, all of which are best effected through a participatory leadership strategy.

Department and Division Heads
Rather than seeking a department head with a typical posting that seeks a "recognized specialist in late-16th-century

Spanish mysticism, scholarly publications essential,'' an appropriate job description for a department head might more reasonably read:

Experienced arbitrator needed to restore effectiveness to divided department. Excellent health, a good sense of humor, practical administrative experience vital; some publications helpful'' (Hilt 1986, p. 80).

Three very distinct types of positions might be identified under the general heading of ''department and division heads.'' These include:

1. The department head in a major university, quite often filled on a rotating basis by senior scholars from within the department, none of whom want the distractions of the job, and each of whom fills it for a two- or three-year term as a professional obligation;
2. The division head, particularly in a community or moderate-sized four-year college, who in actuality may be filling many of the roles of a deanship but with a different title;
3. The department head within a divisional structure, filled sometimes as a very first step in an administrative career ladder, sometimes for titular and some additional financial recognition of the lead teacher in a small department, and sometimes used as a haven for very senior faculty members where less direct classroom contact with students is in everyone's best interest.

Tucker suggests that, in baccalaureate institutions ''department chairpersons perceive themselves primarily as faculty members with some administrative responsibilities,'' while in two-year colleges it is the reverse (1984 p. 30). Summarizing research on what department chairs do, Booth (1982) indicates that chairs in comprehensive universities spend about 21 hours per week in departmental administration, including recordkeeping, budgets, physical facilities, personnel management including faculty development, and liaison duties.

''In assessing the essential qualifications of an effective chairman, I would put intuitive integrity first'' (Brown

. . . Selected candidates had more, and more prestigious, publications than did the faculty members selecting them.

1977, p. 190). Additional qualifications listed by Brown include: a sense of organization; a sense of balance between organization and scholarship; humility to seek advice and to delegate; a willingness to accept responsibility when decisions must be reached; artful leadership; a willingness to assure a proper balance in the diverse approaches to learning and the varied subareas of instruction within the discipline. Burke notes that "participatory management requires a skilled leader (chairman) for optimum results" (1986 p. 6), and she suggests that:

Selection of chairmen who can lead a department to consensus, and chairmen who can develop the environment of mutual trust and shared goals where consensual behavior thrives, is crucial (1986, p. 29).

Other Campus Administrators
Fisher (1985) examines the managerially valuable but little-studied role of the presidental assistant. He suggests that the presidential assistant is an extension of the personality and role of the president; needs the president's complete confidence and to be consistently involved in the presidential business; fills a function that is defined exclusively in terms of the president's best interests. There may not be the slightest appearance of threat to the president or vice presidents. The person must be able to subordinate his or her ego, be available as a confidant(e) to the president, function without power in her/his own right, respect the president, and be able to handle feelings of being lonely, isolated, and invisible. Some of the key characteristics of the good presidential assistant include altruism; an ability to perceive reality and accept it; being able to develop deep interpersonal relationships with others; knowing that an institution does not have the capacity to care or return affection—only people do; and being able to laugh a lot, mostly at oneself, as well as being able to see the fun in any situation (Fisher 1985).

Simmons (1983) has written about the particular roles and responsibilities of administrative officers in small colleges. Noting that the small college president is generally away from campus between one-third and one-half of the time, she suggests that much of the day-to-day management is delegated to vice-presidential level officers, who "must command the respect not only of the president but of the college community;" the majority must be "articulate spokesmen for the college;" at least one "should have familiarity with data analysis;" they must be able to gather intelligence for the president in her or his absence, and be able and willing to provide uncensored information upon the president's return. She also suggests that, in the small college, flexibility and a willingness to work far beyond the normal scope of any given job description, particularly at the middle management level, is critical to the welfare of the enterprise.

Bussey (1981) suggests that the qualifications for a successful college alumni director include having good people skills, dedication, enthusiasm, honesty, good communication skills, humility, and the ability to manage money well.

In addition to a knowledge of basic fiscal management, the qualifications for administrators in finance positions should include good verbal ability, attention to detail, and an ability to see the overall picture (Fear 1984).

Finally, the overall importance of building a presidential team is central to the success of the chief administrative officer. Uehling (1981) suggests that the key characteristics of such a team should include: individuals whose strengths complement the president's and each other's; a balance between those who are fast-moving and those who are deliberate, and between those with task orientations and those with people orientations, as well as between idealists and pragmatists. Uehling also notes that waiting for the right candidate can be painful, but selecting the wrong candidate can be even more costly. And, "in the last analysis, the president decides who the members of the team will be" (p. 28).

Placement specialists often remind us that there are no perfect candidates, and no ideal jobs. The context and conditions of the campus, recent college and larger world history, and the characteristics of candidates must jointly be assessed. It is perhaps possible to derive a general sense that, no matter what the position, search committees need to seek a humane person, someone who is able in interpersonal dealings, with personal integrity that is evidenced in previous work, and with at least some ability to handle the financial and technical aspects of organizational management.

REFERENCES

One of the most difficult arenas to discuss adequately in the search and selection process relates to seeking, securing, and evaluating meaningful and reliable references.

In "the best of all possible worlds," we might be able to seek and obtain written references which are accurate in their assessments, indicate both the strengths and the shortcomings of the candidates, and provide detailed support thereof. For a number of reasons, we do not find ourselves in that world. Levine, reporting the results of a survey of corporate personnel managers, indicated that the two most popular areas of formal inquiries made of previous employers are the dates of employment and whether the employee would be eligible for rehire (1984, p. 9). Most personnel officers "are reluctant to release some or all information" to others about their former employees, yet they "seek the same information when they are hiring. The reason for this 'give little, ask much' practice was caution, not deceit," and a fear of libel suits (Zippo and Greenberg 1982, p. 52).

It was also reported that "78 percent include on their application forms a place where applicants can indicate that they grant the prospective employer permission to check references" (Levine 1984, p. 9). This practice supports the belief that, if applicants have signed such an authorization, they are more likely to tell the truth, particularly since such statements usually include a clause that gives permission to end consideration for employment, or to terminate after employment starts, if there has been any misrepresentation on the application (Fear 1983, p. 76; Vecchio 1984, p. 26).

Written References
In this litigious age, referees rarely write about anything but the positive aspects of a candidate. Occasionally, the perceptive reader of a reference can discern some of what is not being said, but even the "between the lines negative" has become less common. The two things that one might reasonably hope for from written references are that (1) thinking and caring referees will provide narrative support for the fine qualities attributed to the candidate, providing at least some solid reason to accept the positives noted; (2) one would be a weak candidate indeed if she or

---

Selecting College and University Personnel

65

he were not able to find at least several people willing to say good things about him or her.

In at least one academic arena letters of reference do appear to carry particular weight: the selection of new faculty members. Burke (1986) found that letters of reference are extremely important as a screening device for new research faculty members, and that the identity of the author of those letters is one key factor in assessing the letters. When members of a search committee are reviewing written letters of recommendation, they might note that:

- *Sometimes a reference reveals more about its writer than about the applicant. . . .*
- *Letters from faculty members, discussing their students, are often written paternalistically regardless of the student's previous background, age, or experience . . .*
- *If a reference is negative, there may be clues that it reflects a hostile personal relationship between its writer and the candidate. If so, is it possible to attribute the fault to the candidate or the writer? Is it possible that the letter was written by a superior piqued that a subordinate may be leaving, either because an equally good replacement would be hard to find or because of jealousy about the prospective promotion? On the other hand, could it be that the negative reference is the only honest one in the bunch?*
- *Positive and important personal attributes that might come through in references include high energy levels and initiative; the quality of scholarship might also be reflected* (Kaplowitz 1973, p. 21).

Seeking Additional Information

Assuming that a candidate has reached a point where she or he is in serious consideration for a position, further information supporting the claims of the candidate, reflecting strengths and weaknesses, and assessing the candidate for the particular position on the particular campus will be needed and sought.

The seeking of references in any format can be fraught with danger—even more so for the candidate than for the search committee, yet with potential problems for each. If references are sought carelessly, for example, a candidate may feel publicly exposed on her or his home campus, and may withdraw from candidacy, weakening the pool of good candidates for the position. While this issue is discussed in greater depth under the topic of confidentiality and openness in the search, the need to respect the confidentiality of candidates cannot be stated too often.

Information on candidates may be sought both from those people suggested as referees, and from others not so named. In either case, the committee needs to ascertain, with each candidate, whether and when referees may be contacted. If a candidate has asked that people on the home campus not be informed of the candidacy, that request for confidence needs to be respected. If a candidate has indicated that a supervisor may be contacted only if the candidate is a finalist for the position, then when the candidate becomes a finalist (one of 3, not of 18), it is appropriate and necessary that the candidate know of that status, and give permission to contact people on the home campus.

Some of the issues at that point include how and from whom to seek references, how to do so discreetly, and how to get references that are helpful and accurate. One approach is to have a consultant involved in the process, and to let the consultant do the reference checking. An advantage of this approach is that the consultant may have a network that allows for more in-depth, yet still discreet, checking than might otherwise be available to a campus. Good consultants are trusted by their contacts, who may tell them real truths that would not be shared with anyone else. Most searches are conducted, however, without the involvement of a consultant.

Some committees assign one member to do the reference checking for each candidate to assure a uniform approach and uniform reporting back to the committee. Others prefer to involve several members of the committee. In either case, an interview which is structured yet which has sufficient open-ended questions for good discussion is recommended; when several different callers are involved, formal structure is necessary.

It is appropriate and generally quite useful to check with the referees named by the candidate as the primary sources of information. Candidates generally will suggest individuals either to whom they have reported, or with whom they've worked as colleagues, and/or, on some occasions, individuals who have reported to them. It is suggested that this last case can reflect a key issue often overlooked by search committees, and yet a very important question for administrative effectiveness: How well does the candidate build a team and develop the people reporting to him or her? Also, in some cases, a candidate's former secretary—particularly an executive secretary or administrative assistant—can provide more thorough and accurate information than any three vice-presidents.

In addition to referees named by the candidate, search committees sometimes feel a need to seek additional information from other sources, independent sources who may confirm or raise questions about the information already gathered. Again, confidentiality can be an issue.

At the stage at which references are being checked, the person's candidacy often can be disclosed to the referee. However, the sometimes more subtle approaches used by consultants also can be used by committees. A good contact is a discreet contact. Frequently, among the members of the committee, one or more people will have friends on the past and/or current campuses of a candidate . . . friends who truly can be trusted, both for accurate information and for an ability to keep a confidence. Such resources can be very helpful, and it is amazing how often a committee contains sufficient resources within itself to check in that way on each final candidate.

Determining performance in positions prior to the current position generally can be done with a bit more comfort—but, even there, confidentiality should be requested from referees. Everyone connected with the search process in more than casual ways has a treasury of horror stories relating to the checking of references. One frequently repeated problem begins when a member of a search committee calls a colleague on a candidate's home campus. The colleague is generally a member of the parallel department, someone with whom a drink might have been shared once at a professional meeting. That colleague's loyalties, reliability, and ability to be discreet are totally unknown. Such calls are invitations to disaster, and in fact have precipitated problems for more than candidate and committee.

When calling about candidates whose confidentiality is important, one approach sometimes used is to suggest that the individual in question has been nominated for the particular position, but is not yet a candidate and may not even know of the committee's interest, and that the committee is calling to determine whether it is appropriate to pursue the candidacy. Quite frequently, as in the case of nominations and/or active recruiting where good prospective candidates have been identified by the search committee, that is the truth; on the other hand, this approach is not helpful or appropriate if the candidate has visited the campus and that visit most likely is known to the referee.

When calling a referee, a search committee caller will generally identify him- or herself, name the position for which the candidate is being considered, and ask if the person can talk at that time or would rather set an appointment to discuss the nominee or candidate. For active candidates, it is appropriate to indicate that the call is being made to verify information given to the committee by the candidate. A list that has been used with some degree of success to conduct reference checks for administrative candidates includes the following questions:

Everyone connected with the search process in more than casual ways has a treasury of horror stories relating to the checking of references.

1. What was the exact title of the position held by the candidate?
2. What did you think of him/her?
3. Did the candidate have responsibility for the supervision of others? How many? How was it handled?
4. How closely was it necessary to supervise the candidate?
5. Was she/he willing to accept responsibility?
6. Did the candidate have any responsibility for policy formation? How was that handled?
7. Did the candidate develop any new plans or programs? Were they effectively developed? Effectively presented?
8. Did the candidate finish what he/she started?
9. How well did the candidate get along with people?
10. Why did she/he leave?
11. Does the candidate have any personal difficulties that might interfere with effectiveness on the job?
12. What are the candidate's outstanding strong points?

13. What are the candidate's weak points? (Kaplowitz 1973, p. 26).

It is important, of course, to listen carefully and actively to the referee. While body language can't be observed, the use of certain voice tones, phrases, and sometimes misdirections can be very telling. In one recent search, a campus head who was called for a reference on his vice-president suggested that, while competent, the vice-president perhaps was not able to make the hard decisions when necessary. When this conversation was reported in detail to the search committee, committee members somehow felt unsatisfied because of something in the manner in which this opinion had been stated. The committee checked further. They found that, in fact, the vice-president was running the institution, and had managed to retain the confidence and support of the faculty while making significant necessary (and "hard") budgetary adjustments.

Occasionally, answers may seem ambiguous, or the referee's opinion of the candidate's suitability for the particular position may be unclear. Often a clear-cut response can be evoked with a summarizing statement that calls for specific agreement or disagreement, for instance, by using the more appropriate of two suggested statements:

I take it that you don't recommend the applicant very highly for the position, or I take it that you recommend the applicant very highly for the position (Fortunato and Waddell 1981, p. 128).

In summary, it is necessary to discreetly, carefully, and thoroughly research candidates.

False Credentials
A separate yet related issue is the question of false claims on resumes. Noting that "most applicants do present their credentials honestly," Vecchio makes several suggestions to help detect deceptions. Items to watch for include:

- Deliberate creation of uncertainty/ambiguity, as "attended 'x' university;"
- Vague, shifted, omitted dates;

- Differences between honors from, and membership in, professional organizations;
- Omissions, abbreviations, peculiar wordings, and/or odd or puzzling inclusions (Vecchio 1984, p. 27).

Several precautionary actions that may be taken include:

- Circulating the applicant's papers among specialists within the field (a norm for academic candidacies, at least);
- Obtaining a work sample (perhaps something the candidate has published, if appropriate);
- Getting documentation such as official transcripts— which must be done for all candidates at the same level to avoid possible charges of bias (securing official transcripts always is recommended before any appointment is made, and, while an irritant to candidates earlier in the screening, is generally an appropriate precautionary step with respect to all finalists);
- Doing reference checks;
- Including the statement about misrepresentations suggested above on the application form (Vecchio 1984, p. 26).

Finally, if *someone* with false credentials slips through, he or she needs to be removed as quickly as the forgery is discovered (Vecchio 1984, p. 27).

INTERVIEWING CANDIDATES

*Hundreds of books, manuals, and articles have
described how a good employment interview should be
conducted. Most of these assume that the interview will
be rational and objective, and produce a sound decision.
But, according to . . . Webster, this is nonsense* (Zippo
and Northart 1983, p. 79).

Arvey and Campion (1982) express some wonder at why
the interview continues to be so popular as a method for
selection when the fragmented research that exists pro-
duces little of value to selectors. While acknowledging that
it is difficult to identify any equally efficient alternative,
their review of available research reflects that:

1. interviews are valid as a work sample of such behavior as sociability and verbal fluency;
2. interviews are not valid in the selection process as
   predictors of job performance, despite the great faith
   that interviewers have in their judgment;
3. interviews do give the interviewer an opportunity to
   sell the job to the candidate.

Nevertheless, as Burke notes, "there is general agreement
that the interview is the pinnacle of the upward climb . . .
the place where the candidate can perform brilliantly or
self-destruct" (1986, p. 14).

We can anticipate the continuation of interviewing as a
key aspect of the selection process in higher education for
several reasons: the sociability of a prospective faculty
member or administrator is of significance to the various
campus constituencies involved; "the interview must be
regarded as a two-way process" (Palmer 1983, p. 34) to
give the candidate an opportunity to assess the particular
campus as a prospective professional home; we in fact do
not have any equally effective alternative. It would seem
appropriate, therefore, to gather the best available wisdom
on how to make the interview as useful and effective a part
of the quest as possible.

The extensive treatment of the interview process by
Fear (1984), which (deservedly) was named by the American Society for Personnel Administrators as the year's
most outstanding human resource management book,
strongly suggests the value of a carefully planned and

---

structured interview. This will enable interviewers to accomplish their two broad objectives, "to develop relevant information and . . . to interpret the information they bring to light" (p. 85). He suggests that interviews seek to ascertain:

> *how diligently they (the candidates) will be willing to work;*
> *whether they are likely to get along well with people;*
> *whether they can adapt to the environment;*
> *whether they can solve complex problems; and*
> *whether they have the potential for leadership* (Fear 1984, p. 86).

To get the answers to those and similar questions, varying approaches are suggested. "The interviewer's questions . . . must be as tough as the problems that will face the executive who gets the job" (Ginsburg 1980, p. 32). Citing such comments as: "It was obviously a setup for the internal candidate . . ." and "I was given 10 minutes in front of a panel of 12, eight of whom said nothing . . .," Palmer (1983) suggests that each aspect of the interview must be handled as a public relations process.

For faculty candidates at research universities, Burke reports a tripartite interview process:

1. A presentation by the candidate to faculty members and graduate students with research interests similar to those of the candidate. Viewed by many as the most important aspect of the interview. Often called the "group professional activity" or "job talk."
2. Individual meetings with current faculty members, during which those faculty members' research and "what life is like" at the institution are frequently discussed; also, meeting with graduate students and, sometimes, with the appropriate dean(s).
3. The semisocial periods, which have "to be considered very semi," as much grilling and testing of "whether the candidate will fit in as a colleague" take place during these times (1986, pp. 15–17).

There appears to be general agreement that good interviewing can and should be taught (Fear 1984; Felton and

Lamb 1982; Goodace 1982; Palmer 1983). On the other hand, the amount of structure recommended for interviews does vary. Bouchard, Deane, and Roots suggest that "a selection interview should be as structured as possible, yet tailored to each particular applicant" (1983, p. 6), while Goodace (1982) prefers a more semistructured approach, with significant amounts of flexibility.

Conducting the Interview
Noting that "the actual moment of entering the room is a daunting one, even for the most experienced candidates," Palmer (1983, p. 36) suggests that the person chairing a group interview rise and shake hands with the candidate, and then introduce the other members of the panel by name and position. As candidates will then "promptly forget these, the use of name cards would be helpful" (p. 37). It has been noted that some members of the campus community, particularly those who may be serving on search committees for the first time, also may approach the first interview(s) with a degree of trepidation.

A typical interview might begin with an attempt to establish informal rapport, then include an explanation of the purpose and agenda, a gathering of information, some description of the job and organization, and time for answering the candidate's questions; it might conclude with an expression of appreciation to the candidate, and an indication of what will happen next in the process (Bouchard, Deane, and Roots, 1983). McVicker (1986) warns that the interviewer(s) need to be well prepared before the interview begins, to have reviewed carefully each candidate's materials before the interview, and to have notes on pertinent information given and desired and specific questions that need to be asked.

To actually gather the desired information, Fear provides a number of detailed recommendations on how key interview tasks might be accomplished; the new interviewer will find his book to be of significant value. In brief, his suggestions include:

1. Seek to have the candidate do as much as 85 percent of the talking, and use carefully worded questions to do so.

2. Exhibit helpful interviewing skills, including appropriate encouraging non-verbal behavior, the judicious use of the calculated pause in listening, encouraging voice tone, and positive verbal and non-verbal reinforcement to appropriately recognize achievements. Soften direct questions with such phrases as: "Is it possible that" . . . "How did you happen to" . . . "Has there been any opportunity to" . . . "To what do you attribute" . . . "might" . . . "perhaps" . . . "to some extent" . . . "somewhat" . . . and "a little bit."

3. Begin with small talk to help the candidate get used to hearing his/her voice in that environment.

4. Bridge the gap between the small talk and the first question with a comment such as, "Let me tell you a little bit about our discussion today"; include an overview of the interview.

5. Ask candidates to talk about the details of each previous job, including duties and responsibilities, job likes and dislikes and any special achievements along the way. "The comprehensive introductory question represents the single most important technique for getting applicants to do most of the talking" (p. 102).

6. Use follow–up questions and comments to help probe more deeply for clues to behavior by examining three key areas of previous jobs: achievements and strengths demonstrated; development needs identified ("Did you get any clues to your development needs as a result of working on those jobs? You know, we all have some shortcomings . . ." (p. 298)); factors that have provided job satisfaction for the individual.

7. "The interview that results in no unfavorable information is inescapably a poor interview" (p. 89). Play down unfavorable information, e.g., saying that a person has faced up to prior problems serves to acknowledge them without making light of them. This will make discussion of areas for growth more acceptable to the candidate. However, if an interviewer "gives the slightest indication that judgment is being adversely influenced by unfavorable infor-

mation . . . (the interviewer) . . . will get no further information of this kind" (pp. 101–102).

8. Don't ask questions that "lead" to a particular answer. "There is a wonderful phrase—'To what extent'—that makes any question open-ended . . .: 'To what extent were you successful on that job?' " (p. 109). Similarly, the question, "How did you feel about that situation?" is a more neutral way of asking a question, and helps get an objective response.

9. Make sparing but judicious use of "Why" questions, because the reasons that an individual took some course of action can tell a great deal about the candidate's judgment and motivation.

10. Construct hypotheses about the candidate's behavior, based on early clues, and then test these hypotheses with probes at appropriate intervals throughout the discussion (1984, pp. 89–121).

Higgins and Hollander suggest that questions in an interview should evoke descriptions of how candidates have behaved in specific situations in the past. "The argument is that past behavior is the best predictor of future behavior" (1987, p. 69). One difficulty with this otherwise valid approach is that it can tend to mitigate toward candidates who have held similar positions in the past. It is much easier unfortunately to hire someone who has already served as a president (even if unsuccessfully) than to hire someone who may have all of the requisite skills but "just hasn't done the job before."

Ginsburg suggests structuring an interview with more pointed questions. He provides a specific listing of 35 questions that he believes an interviewer should ask, and he offers 25 questions that the interviewer might expect to be asked by a candidate who "tests reality aggressively" (1980, p. 34). A typical Ginsburg question to a candidate is:

I assume that at some point you were in head-on competition with an individual . . . for promotion or status or . . . something of that type. What would your competitor say about you in terms of your strengths and weaknesses?" (p. 33).

Ginsburg suggests that good candidates can be expected to include such questions as "What are the strengths and weaknesses of my prospective subordinates?'' (p. 35), and, ''Why did my predecessor leave the position, what were her or his strengths, weaknesses, accomplishments, failures?'' (p. 36). In academia, good candidates generally tend to be asking those same questions, but rather more indirectly than directly. The good candidate generally will have the answers to those questions by the end of a day of campus-based interviewing, more often as a result of good listening and indirect questioning than of asking the more direct questions suggested by Ginsburg.

Questions about likes and dislikes on a job can generate many valuable clues: ''discussion of reasons for leaving jobs may provide clues to assets . . . (and/or to) . . . liabilities'' (Fear 1984, p. 192). However, examining the reasons for changing jobs

> *. . . is one of the most delicate aspects of the interview, since many applicants are sensitive about their reasons for having left certain jobs. Therefore, we try to get this information spontaneously and indirectly by probing for job dislikes. If this fails, however, we have to approach the situation more directly with a softened follow-up question such as, ''How did you happen to leave that job?'' In posing this question, the interviewer should, of course, give particular attention to her facial expressions and vocal intonation, in order to give an appearance of seeming as disarming and permissive as possible* (Fear 1984, p. 190).

In asking questions during an interview, it is important to remember Equal Employment Opportunity considerations, i.e., keep questions job related; do not ask questions of women or minority group members that would not be asked of others; do not ask women (and men) about plans for marriage, children, or childcare; do not ask older candidates about retirement plans (Fear 1984). Other topics generally considered inappropriate, and in some cases illegal, are sexual preference, religion, national origins, handicaps, and age (Bouchard, Deane, and Roots 1983).

> *And for heaven's sake, don't try to trick the applicant into giving you information or coyly say, ''I know I'm not supposed to ask this, but. . . .'' A smart applicant*

*will reply, "You're right, you're not!" and cross you off
the list of possibilities* (McVicker 1986, p. 68).

When a candidate comes to a campus for an interview,
that candidate is considering a cluster of major changes in
her or his life, including new responsibilities, frequently
including a new geographic location and distancing from
existing social and professional support systems, and often
including similar relocation issues for family members as
well. Candidates expose themselves, to allow interviewers
to examine, and then pass judgment, on the very central
professional and personal elements of their lives. Interviews are structured to allow and help members of search
committees extract and examine the pertinent information
on candidates, to help examine the fit between those candidates and the campus context. Particularly because candidates have made themselves open in this process, members
of the search committee must demonstrate the highest levels of personal and professional courtesy and consideration
to all of their candidates in both the formal and informal
portions of candidates' visits and interviews.

While the personnel function on campus historically has been quite separate from the academic endeavor, such factors as the complex legal and statistical aspects of affirmative action, the increased formalization of recordkeeping and decision making, the greater complexity and centralization of benefits administration, and the availability on campus of increasingly able personnel professionals have begun to blur some of the lines between academic and nonacademic personnel administration.

A key work (Fortunado and Waddell 1981) provides a comprehensive treatment of the traditional roles and responsibilities of the personnel administration function in the context of higher education, including wage and salary management, position analysis, employment, affirmative action, benefits, development, and personnel recordkeeping.

The employment function of the personnel office focuses primarily on the recruitment of campus support staff.

The employment function of the personnel office focuses primarily on the recruitment of campus support staff. In general, support personnel on a campus are a caring, hardworking, and valuable component of the academic enterprise. They provide assistance to faculty members in the preparation of course materials and of manuscripts reporting research findings; they often represent availability and continuity to students; and they are generally a major transmitter of a given campus' tone and culture.

A detailed discussion of the recruitment and selection of support personnel, which is beyond the purview of this book, is found in Fortunado and Waddell (1981, pp. 86–139). Additionally, the College and University Personnel Association provides much useful and timely material in its journals. A third major resource for the recruitment and selection of support staff is the staffing section of the comprehensive corporate sector handbook published by the American Society for Personnel Administration (Yoder and Heneman, Jr., editors, 1979, pp. 4.1–4.296; updates of the handbook are scheduled for release in six parts, to be published twice a year beginning in the fall of 1987).

With respect to academic staffing, the role of personnel officers will vary from campus to campus. "Intruders" into the academic arena occasionally are met with hostility. In cases where the chief personnel administrator and/or the affirmative action officer have become the campus experts on the search process, and are able and willing to provide both technical and recordkeeping assistance, faculty hostility has turned into an appreciative welcome. In some cases, personnel and/or affirmative action officers hold an ex-officio slot on search committees. It follows, of course, that the personnel officers serve to help with the technical process, and they do not seek to intrude on the judgments of academic competence. Personnel and affirmative action offices that are structured to use computers for record keeping and for word processing can also provide that kind of support in academic searches.

Additionally, the personnel office can be of particular assistance in the preparation of materials for candidates for all positions. Some of the information needed by presidential candidates, such as a true picture of the institution's fiscal situation and the depth of alumni support (Mundinger 1982), will come from the board. On the other hand, a sense of the campus and its community very helpfully can be gathered by, and be available from, the personnel office for all candidates for employment at the college.

Salary information is an area that is extremely delicate on some campuses, and yet is open and published on others. Where that information is in the public domain, perhaps in the form of salary schedules, having the schedules available through a personnel office can be extremely helpful to the search committee. Similarly, a package describing health, retirement, and related benefits generally is much more comprehensively gathered by personnel people than by academics.

The personnel officer can be of further help in the broader area of salary administration by maintaining current information on faculty and administrative salaries in comparable colleges both nationally and regionally. If administrators and librarians are alerted to assist, the personnel office also could maintain current articles on related topics, including presidential pay levels (Manley 1984), the current year's copy of the Association of American University Professors annual edition of *Academe* that focuses on the economic status of the profession, copies of College and University Personnel Association salary studies, etc. A file of studies on the costs for hiring academic administrators also would be of interest. For example, the study by Dingerson, Rodman, and Wade (1982) reflects a (by now long outdated) mean cost of $8,631 to fill selected academic positions.

In summary, then, the personnel office can play an increasingly helpful support role in the selection of academic personnel on campus.

SUMMARY AND IMPLICATIONS

The selection of the faculty and the administrative leadership on campus is at the very heart of the future of the academic enterprise. It therefore appears imperative to recruit and hire the finest people possible. This chapter addresses two kinds of issues—the practical issues that can make the search process effective and efficient, and the related larger societal issues.

The use of the search committee in the selection of campus leaders has evolved into an almost hallowed approach. There are many positive results of the committee process; several issues, however, need to be addressed so that the potential pitfalls can be avoided while the maximum good is obtained.

1. Careful thought and planning are necessary before a search committee is convened. It is important to ensure that the board of trustees (for a president) or the president will have and maintain the ultimate responsibility for the selection and appointment of administrators on campus. At the same time, affected constituencies need to have a sense that their legitimate concerns are being heard and listened to. Recognizing the strong thrust for confidentiality once the search begins, it is necessary to ensure a process for the selection of committee members that will generate a committee whose members are trusted by the various constituencies.

2. Once the committee is structured, its policies and procedures should be clear, and clearly transmitted to the campus at large. Similarly, the position should be posted as broadly as possible.

3. There is a considerable difference, however, between public disclosure of procedures and the need to maintain confidentiality, particularly in presidential and vice-presidential searches, if a full range of top candidates is to be developed. It is important for the committee members and for the campus at large to be reminded, probably several times, of the need for, and the value of, confidentiality.

4. Committees need to seek out candidates for vacancies actively and aggressively. In some cases, the best candidates indicate their interest in the position themselves; in others, the best candidates are happily at

work in another position, and are not even thinking about the possibility of moving to another job. Casting out a wide net, through a range of postings, contacts, and conversations, will produce the best candidate pool.

5. The pool of able and capable female administrators and faculty members has increased significantly over the past 15 years, and there is no reason to anticipate any change in that development. Reaching out to locate those women, and evaluating them against the needs of the position rather than against an outdated notion of resume experience, is important if a full range of roles is to be filled, and a full range of role models is to be available.

6. The pool of available members of minority groups is less large, which makes it all the more important to actively and affirmatively seek and find good administrators and faculty members in that pool.

7. When a candidate is invited to a campus for an interview, in-depth two-way interviewing is important if the selection is to be based on the qualities needed for that campus rather than on a slick or showy style.

8. Similarly, reference checks are important to determine whether a candidate has the strength and courage to reach out and try, and to survive some failures, and to keep trying, without ever losing sight of the individual people who are the most important part of any organization.

9. Additional formal research on selected aspects of the search and selection process in higher education could be very helpful. Three particular areas in which such research and literature are sparse to non-existent are: the dynamics and politics of the process of selecting and appointing one person from among several final candidates; factors which can maximize the efficacy of interviews; issues relating to the selection and subsequent success of internal vs. external candidates.

Two larger societal issues also need to be addressed. There is a need for multiphasic attention to actively develop the talent and abilities that are not adequately coming to maturation in our minority populations. If we are to have a broadly constituted faculty in 25 years, now is the time to increase broadly based social efforts to reach and nurture that future faculty.

There is, additionally, a need to develop allies with common concerns about the limitations on personnel practices that result from the legal requirement in some states to hold discussions of personnel issues "in the sunshine." The old, secret ways of doing business, too often, were quite far from the best interests of the public. Sunshine laws are clearly intended to be, and for the most part very much are, in the public interest. Good leadership from within public higher education, working with other comparably concerned public agencies, is needed, however, to seek legislative re-examination of that aspect of some sunshine laws that requires the public listing of candidates, and public discussions about the professional and personal reputations of those candidates.

When the hero-quest has been accomplished . . . the norm of the monomyth requires that the hero shall now begin the labor of bringing the runes of wisdom . . . back into the kingdom of humanity, where the boon may redound to the renewing of the community . . . (Campbell 1968, p. 193).

The conclusion of a successful search is only the beginning of a new phase of the life cycle of a campus. May all of your quests and journeys be successful!

REFERENCES

The ERIC Clearinghouse on Higher Education abstracts and indexes the current literature on higher education for the Office of Educational Research and Improvement's monthly bibliographic journal, *Resources in Education*. Most of these publications are available through the ERIC Document Reproduction Service (EDRS). For publications cited in this bibliography that are available from EDRS, ordering number and price are included. Readers who wish to order a publication should write to the ERIC Document Reproduction Service, 3900 Wheeler Avenue, Alexandria, Virginia, 22304. When ordering, please specify the document number. Documents are available as noted in microfiche (MF) and paper copy (PC). Because prices are subject to change, it is advisable to check the latest issue of *Resources in Education* for current cost based on the number of pages in the publication.

American Association of University Professors. 1981. "Faculty Participation in the Selection, Evaluation, and Retention of Administrators." *Academe* 67(5): 323–24.

Arvey, R.D.; and Campion, J.E. 1982. "The Employment Interview: A Summary and Review of Recent Research." *Personnel Psychology* 35.

Ashworth, Kenneth H. 1982. "Searching, Searching, Gone. Will Public Disclosure of Presidential Search Proceedings Drive Candidates Away?" *Change* 14(3): 20–23.

Bartlett, Bertrice, and Barnes, Elizabeth. 1978. "Women's Vitae and the Problem of Perceiving Competence." Position Paper. ED 192 048. 45 pp. MF–$1.00; PC–$5.44.

Bergmann, Barbara R. 1985. " 'Comparable Worth' for Professors." *Academe* 71(4): 8–10.

Bettelheim, Bruno. 1977. *The Uses of Enchantment*. New York: Vintage Books.

Bisesi, Michael. 1985. "Presidential Search: Four Specific Tasks." *AGB Reports* 27(2): 22–23.

Booth, David B. 1982. *The Department Chair*. AAHE-ERIC/ Higher Education Report No. 10, Washington, D.C.: American Association for Higher Education. ED 226 689. 60 pp. MF–$1.00; PC–$7.29.

Bouchard, Ronald A.; Deane, Nancy H.; and Roots, David R. 1983. *Interview Guide For Supervisors*. Washington, D.C.: College and University Personnel Association.

Brown, David G., ed. 1984. *Leadership Roles of Chief Academic Officers*. New Directions for Higher Education No. 47, San Francisco: Jossey–Bass.

Brown, J. Douglas. 1977. "Departmental and University Leadership." In *Academic Departments,* edited by Dean E. McHenry. San Francisco: Jossey–Bass.

Burke, Dolores L. 1986. "In Search of the Best: Junior Faculty Recruitment in American Research Universities." Witzenhausen/Dohrenbach: Paper presented at the Fifth International Seminar on Staff, Program and Organizational Development in Higher Education.

Bussey, Rodney C. 1981. "How to Hire: Alumni Relations Director." *CASE Currents* 8(8): 26–27.

Campbell, Joseph. 1968. *The Hero With A Thousand Faces*. 2d ed. Princeton: Princeton University Press.

Carpenter, Don A. 1979. "Presidential Search, Utah Style." *AGB Reports* 21(5): 13–18.

Cleveland, Harlan. 1985. *The Costs and Benefits of Openness*. Washington, D.C.: Association of Governing Boards of Universities and Colleges.

De Zonia, Robert H. 1979. "Acting Presidents Should Act Like Presidents." *AGB Reports* 21(6): 32–36.

Dingerson, Michael R.; Rodman, John A.; and Wade, John F. 1982. "Procedures and Costs for Hiring Academic Administrators." *Journal of Higher Education* 53(1): 63–74.

Eaton, Judith S. June 1984. "Tapping Neglected Leadership Sources." In *Emerging Roles for Community College Leaders*, edited by Richard L. Alfred, Paul A. Elsner, R. Jan LeCroy, and Nancy Armes. New Directions for Community Colleges No. 46, San Francisco: Jossey–Bass.

Ernst, Richard J. 1982. "Women in Higher Education Leadership Positions—It Doesn't Happen by Accident." *Journal of the College and University Personnel Association* 33(2): 19–22.

Evangelauf, Jean. May 14, 1986. "Professors in High–Demand Fields are Getting Higher–Than–Average Salaries, 2 Studies Find." *The Chronicle of Higher Education* 32(11): 25, 28.

Evans, Nancy J., and Kuh, George D. Spring 1983. "Getting to the Top: A Profile of Female Chief Student Affairs Officers." *Journal of the National Association for Women Deans, Administrators, and Counselors* 46(3): 18–22.

Fear, Richard A. 1984. *The Evaluation Interview*. 3d ed. New York: McGraw–Hill.

Felicetti, Daniel A. 1984. "The Search Process: The Candidate's Perspective on Avoiding Common Institutional Errors." San Francisco: Paper presented at the Conference on Post–secondary Education. ED 251 056. 26 pp. MF–$1.00; PC–$5.44.

Felton, Barbara, and Lamb, Sue R. 1982. "A Model for Systematic Selection Interviewing." *Personnel* 59(1): 40–48.

Fields, Cheryl M. May 28, 1986a. "High Court Backs Affirmative Action in Certain Forms." *The Chronicle of Higher Education* 32(13): 1, 15–18.

————. June 4, 1986b. "Justice Department Official Says High–Court Ruling Requires Repeal of Affirmative Action Order." *The Chronicle of Higher Education* 32(14): 10.

Finlay, Cheryl S., and Crosson, Patricia H. 1981. "Women in Higher Education Administration: Status and Strategies." *Administrator's Update* 2(3): 1–7. ED 200 120. 7 pp. MF–$1.00; PC–$3.59.

Fisher, James L. 1984. *Power of the Presidency*. New York: American Council on Education/Macmillan.

————. 1985. "Presidential Assistants: An Unsung Resource." *AGB Reports* 27(6): 33–36.

Flake, Carol. 1986. "While You're Alive, Be Alive." Myrtle Beach, S.C.: Paper presented at USC/Coastal Carolina College's "Expo '86."

Fortunato, Ray T., and Waddell, D. Geneva. 1981. *Personnel Administration in Higher Education*. San Francisco: Jossey–Bass.

Freeman, Lewis. 1985. "Changes in Membership of Search Committees and College Presidential Qualifications." Unpublished paper. New York: Columbia University.

Friedman, Robert S. 1983. "Presidential Selection: Making It Work." *AGB Reports* 25(5): 44–46.

Gale, Robert. 1980. "Foreword." *Presidential Search,* by John W. Nason. Washington, D.C.: Association of Governing Boards of Universities and Colleges.

Gappa, Judith M. 1984. *Part–Time Faculty: Higher Education at a Crossroads*. ASHE-ERIC/Higher Education Report No. 3, Washington, D.C.: Association for the Study of Higher Education. ED 251 058. 129 pp. MF–$1.00; PC–$12.84.

Gelbspan, Ross, and Kaufman, Jonathan. Nov. 11, 1985. "Blacks Faring Better in Trade Unions Than On Campuses." *Boston Globe* 228(134): 1, 18.

Ghaemmaghami, Sedigheh. 1984. "Faculty Perceptions of an Ideal College President in Oklahoma's Public Four–Year Colleges." Ed.D. dissertation, Oklahoma State University. Reported in *Dissertation Abstracts International*. November 1985. 46(05): 1203A.

Gilley, J. Wade; Fulmer, Kenneth A.; and Reithlingshoefer, Sally J. 1986. *Searching for Academic Excellence*. New York: Macmillan.

Ginsburg, Sigmund G. 1980. "Preparing for Executive Position Interviews: Questions the Interviewer Might Ask—or Be Asked." *Personnel* 57(4): 31–36.

Goodace, James G. 1982. *The Fine Art of Interviewing*. New York: Prentice Hall.

Green, Madeleine F. 1986. "Presidential Leadership: Changes in Style." *AGB Reports* 28(1): 18–20.

Hankin, Joseph N. 1984. "Affirmative Action in Two–Year Colleges, 1983–1984." Cambridge: Paper presented at the National Conference on Issues Facing Black Administrators at Predominantly White Colleges and Universities. ED 244 710. 10 pp. MF–$1.00; PC–$3.59.

———. 1985. "Where the (Affirmative) Action Is (or Is Not): The Status of Minorities and Women Among the Faculty and Administrators of Public Two–Year Colleges, 1983–84." Orlando, Fla.: Paper presented at the annual National Conference of the College and University Personnel Association.

Hansen, W. Lee. 1985. "Salary Differences Across Disciplines." *Academe* 71(4): 6–7.

Hartley, Joyce F., and Ness, Frederic W. 1981. "The Presidential Search Service." *AGB Reports* 23(1): 37–39.

Heald, James E. 1982. "Education Deans and Their Selection." *Journal of Teacher Education* 33(1): 47–49.

Healy, Timothy S. 1985. "Looking for 'God on a Good Day.' " *AGB Reports* 27(2): 22–23.

Heller, Scott. June 26, 1985. "Colleges Trying 'Vita Banks' as a Tool to Attract Minority Candidates for Jobs." *The Chronicle of Higher Education* 30(17): 17, 20.

Higgins, John M., and Hollander, Patricia A. 1987. *A Guide to Successful Searches for College Personnel*. Asheville: College Administration Publications.

Hilt, Douglas. April 30, 1986. "More Collegiality Could Foster Civilized Behavior in Academe." *The Chronicle of Higher Education* 32(9): 80.

Hixson, Vivian S. July 17, 1985. "Cartoon." *The Chronicle of Higher Education.* 30(20): 33.

Huckle, Patricia. Fall 1983. "A Decade's Difference: Mid–Level Managers and Affirmative Action." *Public Personnel Management* 12(3): 249–257.

Hyer, Patricia B. May/June 1985. "Affirmative Action for Women Faculty: Case Studies of Three Successful Institutions." *The Journal of Higher Education* 56(3): 282–299.

Kaffer, Robert E. September/October 1981. "Presidential Search: How to Ruin It." *AGB Reports* 23(5): 16–18.

Kamen, Al, and Marcus, Ruth. July 3, 1986. "Race–based Hiring Plans are Upheld." *Boston Globe* 230(3): 1, 6.

Kantor, Rosabeth M., and Wheatley, Margaret J. 1978. "Women in Higher Education Administration." *Carnegie Corporation Report Summary*. Washington: Association of American Colleges. ED 162 572. 8 pp. MF–$1.00; PC–$3.59.

Kaplowitz, Richard A. 1973. *Selecting Academic Administrators: The Search Committee*. Washington: American Council on Education.

———. 1977. "Recruitment, Appointment, Promotion, and Termination of Academic Personnel." In *The International Encyclopedia of Higher Education*. Asa S. Knowles, editor in chief. San Francisco: Jossey–Bass.

———. 1978. "The Impact of Sunshine/Open Meeting Laws on the Governing Boards of Public Colleges and Universities." Position Paper, prepared for the Association of Governing Boards of Universities and Colleges. ED 272 059. 33 pp. MF–$1.00; PC–$5.44.

Kauffman, Joseph F. 1974. *The Selection of College and University Presidents*. Washington: Association of American Colleges.

———. 1978. "Strategies for Identifying and Advancing Women in Higher Education." Chicago: AAHE Panel. ED 166 998. 7 pp. MF–$1.00; PC–$3.59.

———. 1980. *At the Pleasure of the Board: The Service of the College and University President*. Washington: American Council on Education. ED 152 406. 122 pp. MF–$1.00; PC–$10.99.

Kemerer, Frank R.; Mensel, Frank; and Baldridge, J. Victor. Spring 1981. "Twilight of Informal Faculty Personnel Procedures." *The Journal of the College and University Personnel Association*. 32(1): 17–25.

Kerr, Clark. 1982. "Crisis in Leadership." *AGB Reports* 24(4): 4–7.

———. 1984. *Leaders Make a Difference*. Washington: Association of Governing Boards of Universities and Colleges.

Kiersh, Ed. September 1979. "Presidential Searches: Divided We Stand." *Change* 11(6): 29–35.

Leslie, David W.; Kellams, Samuel E.; and Gunne, G. Manny. 1982. *Part–Time Faculty in American Higher Education*. New York: Praeger.

Levine, Hermine Z. 1984. "Consensus: Report on the October 1983 Questionnaire." *Personnel Magazine* 61(1): 6–9.

Libby, Patricia A. 1983. *In Search of a Community College President*. Annandale: Association of Community Colleges. ED 229 067. 41 pp. MF–$1.00; PC–$5.44.

Lutz, Frank W. 1979. "The Governance Implications of Deanship Selection: And Other Selected Thoughts on the Process." Research report. University Park: Pennsylvania State University. ED 174 135. 23 pp. MF–$1.00; PC–$3.59.

MacTavish, Margaret. 1984. "Defining and Locating Effective Leaders." In *Emerging Roles for Community College Leaders,* edited by Richard L. Alfred, Paul A. Elsner, R. Jan LeCroy, and Nancy Armes. New Directions for Community Colleges No. 46, San Francisco: Jossey–Bass.

Manley, Frank. September/October 1984. "Presidential Pay: Not Exactly Lavish." *AGB Reports* 26(5): 36–39.

Mayhew, Lewis B. 1979. *Surviving the Eighties*. San Francisco: Jossey–Bass.

McCall, Morgan W., Jr., and Lombardo, Michael M. February 1983. "What Makes a Top Executive?" *Psychology Today* 17(2): 26–31.

McLaughlin, Judith B. 1983. "Confidentiality and Disclosure in the Presidential Search." Ed.D. dissertation, Harvard University.

––––––. March 1985a. "From Secrecy to Sunshine: An Overview of Presidential Search Practice." *Journal of the Association for Institutional Research* 22(2): 195–208.

––––––. May/June 1985b. "Plugging Search Committee Leaks." *AGB Reports* 27(2): 24–30.

McLaughlin, Judith B., and Riesman, David. Summer 1985. "The Vicissitudes of the Search Process." *Journal of the Association for the Study of Higher Education* 8(4): 341–355.

––––––. Summer 1986. "The Shady Side of Sunshine." *Teachers College Record* 87(4): 471–494.

McMillen, Liz. Nov. 5, 1986a. "Most Effective College Presidents are 'Risk Takers' Who Rely on Respect, Not Popularity, Study Finds." *The Chronicle of Higher Education* 33(10): 11, 13.

––––––. Dec. 3, 1986b. "Women's Groups: Going the Old Boys' Network One Better." *The Chronicle of Higher Education* 33(14): 15–17.

McMillen, Liz, and Heller, Scott. Sept. 10, 1986. "Women Flock to Graduate School in Record Numbers, but Fewer Blacks are Entering the Academic Pipeline." *The Chronicle of Higher Education* 33(2): 1, 25–26.

McVicker, Mary Frech. December 1986. "The Seven Deadly Sins of Interviewing." *Pace* 13(12): 67–69.

Moore, Kathryn M. 1982. "What to do Until the Mentor Arrives? Professional Advancement Kit." Washington, D.C.: Position Paper prepared for the National Association for Women Deans, Administrators, and Counselors. ED 234 296. 14 pp. MF–$1.00; PC–not available EDRS.

Mortimer, Kenneth. 1986. "Academic Staffing: Be Flexible and Fair." *AGB Reports* 28(2): 29–31.

Mortimer, Kenneth; Bagshaw, Marque; and Masland, Andrew. 1985. *Flexibility in Academic Staffing: Effective Policies and*

Practices. ASHE-ERIC Higher Education Report No. 1, Washington, D.C.: Association for the Study of Higher Education. ED 260 67. 121 pp. MF–$1.00; PC–$10.99.

Mottram, Richard A. Winter 1983. "Executive Search Firms as an Alternative to Search Committees." *Educational Record* 64(1): 38–40.

Mundinger, Donald C. 1982. "What a Presidential Candidate Needs to Know." *AGB Reports* 24(2): 41–45.

Nason, John W. 1980. *Presidential Search*. Washington: Association of Governing Boards of Universities and Colleges. ED 238 358. 94 pp. MF–$1.00; PC–not available EDRS.

———. 1984. *Presidential Search*. Revised Ed. Washington: Association of Governing Boards of Universities and Colleges. ED 247 877. 122 pp. MF–$1.00; PC–not available EDRS.

Palmer, Robin. 1983. "A Sharper Focus on the Panel Interview." *Personnel Management* 15(5): 34–37.

Parsons, Michael H., ed. 1980. *Using Part–Time Faculty Effectively*. New Directions for Community Colleges No. 30, San Francisco: Jossey–Bass.

Perry, Robert H. 1984. *How To Answer a Headhunter's Call*. New York: American Management Associations.

Porter, Earl W. 1983. "The Presidential Search as the Presidents See It." *AGB Reports* 25(1): 43–47.

Pray, Francis C. 1979. "The President as 'Reasonable Adventurer.' " *AGB Reports* 21(3): 45–48. EJ 205 040.

Query, Lance. 1985. "Librarians and Teaching Faculty: Disparity Within the System." *Academe* 71(4): 13–16.

Reid, John Y., and Rogers, Sharon J. 1981. "The Search for Academic Leadership: Selecting Chief Academic Officers in American Colleges and Universities." Washington, D.C.: Paper presented at a meeting of the Association for the Study of Higher Education. ED 203 801. 12 pp. MF–$1.00; PC–$3.59.

Reynolds, Pamela. June 25, 1986. "Accentuating the Affirmative." *Boston Globe* 229(360): 41.

Riesman, David, and McLaughlin, Judith B. 1984. "A Primer on the Use of Consultants in Presidential Recruitment." *Change* 16(6): 12–23.

Rivera, Manuel G. 1983. "Hispanic Participation in the Administration of the California Community Colleges: 1981–82." Fresno, Calif.: Paper presented at the Annual Conference of the Association of Mexican American Educators. ED 238 622. 44 pp. MF–$1.00; PC–not available EDRS.

Rodman, John A., and Dingerson, Michael R. 1986. "University Hiring Practices for Academic Administrators." *The Journal of the College and University Personnel Association* 37(2): 24–30.

Rosovsky, Henry. 1987. "Deaning." *Harvard Magazine* 89(3): 34–40.

Rubenfeld, Stephen, and Crino, Michael. 1981. "Are Employment Agencies Jeopardizing Your Selection Process?" *Personnel* 58(5): 70–77.

Sagaria, Mary Ann D., and Krotseng, Marsha V. 1986. "Deans' Managerial Skills: What They Need and What They Bring to the Job." *The Journal of the College and University Personnel Association* 37(2): 1–6.

Shepard, Ira M. July 21, 1986. "Supreme Court Affirms Affirmative Action Remedies Under Title VII." *Personnelite*. College and University Personnel Association. 13(22): 1.

Sherman, Malcolm J. July 3, 1985. "The Controversial Theory of 'Comparable Worth' on College Campuses." *The Chronicle of Higher Education* 30(18): 64.

Simmons, Adele. 1983. "Organizing and Staffing a Small College." In *Management Techniques for Small and Specialized Institutions,* edited by Andrew J. Falender and John C. Merson. New Directions for Higher Education No. 42, San Francisco: Jossey–Bass.

Skipper, Charles E. 1982. "Four Indicators of Administrative Effectiveness." Paper. New York: American Educational Research Association. ED 216 634. 8 pp. MF–$1.00; PC–$3.59.

Sojka, Gary A. 1985. "An Administrator's View: Balancing Academic Performance and Market Conditions." *Academe* 71(4): 11–12.

Stead, Ronald. 1985. "UpFront." *AGB Reports* 27(3): 2–3.

Stent, Angela. 1978. "Academe's New Girl Network." *Change* 10(6): 18–21.

Stewart, Robert; Stickler, I. Bruce; and Abcarian, Michael V. 1985. "Complying with Affirmative Action in 1985." *The CEO Management Letter Update* 5(10): 1, 4–6.

Strider, Robert L. 1981. "Memo to a Search Committee." *AGB Reports* 23(1): 32–36.

Taylor, Robert A. 1984. *How to Select and Use an Executive Search Firm.* New York: McGraw–Hill.

Thompson, Patricia, and Thompson, Hugh. 1983. "One for the Money, Two for the Show." *AGB Reports* 25(3): 44–46.

Townsend, Barbara K. May 28, 1986. "Outsiders Inside Academe: The Plight of Temporary Teachers." *The Chronicle of Higher Education* 32(13): 72.

Trachtenberg, Stephen J. 1981. "Not What It's Cracked Up to Be." In *Academic Leaders as Managers,* edited by Robert H. Atwell and Madeleine F. Green. New Directions for Higher Education No. 36, San Francisco: Jossey–Bass.

Tucker, A. 1984. *Chairing the Academic Department: Leadership Among Peers*. New York: Macmillan.

Uehling, Barbara S. 1981. "Building a Presidential Team." In *Academic Leaders as Managers,* edited by Robert H. Atwell and Madeleine F. Green. New Directions for Higher Education No. 36, San Francisco: Jossey–Bass.

VanderWaerdt, Lois. 1982. *Affirmative Action in Higher Education—A Sourcebook*. New York: Garland.

Vecchio, Robert P. 1984. "The Problem of Phony Resumes: How to Spot a Ringer Among the Applicants." *Personnel* 61(2): 22–27.

Walker, Donald E. 1979. *The Effective Administrator*. San Francisco: Jossey–Bass.

Watkins, Beverly T. July 17, 1985. "Court Orders University to Give Faculty Union and Anti–Bias Officer Power to Veto Job Offers." *The Chronicle of Higher Education* 30(20): 23–25.

———. June 4, 1986. "Successful Colleges Found Headed by Presidents Who Are 'People Oriented,' Doggedly Persistent." *The Chronicle of Higher Education* 32(14): 1, 22.

Wilson, Reginald. 1985. "Affirmative Action: The Current Status." *AGB Reports* 27(3): 17–21.

Winkler, Karen J. May 29, 1985. " 'Sunshine' Laws Less Harmful to Colleges than Report Charged, Critics Say." *The Chronicle of Higher Education* 30(13): 13.

Yoder, Dale, and Heneman, Herbert G., Jr. 1979. *ASPA Handbook of Personnel and Industrial Relations*. Washington: The Bureau of National Affairs.

Zippo, Mary. September 1980. "Getting the Most Out Of An Executive Search Firm." *Personnel* 57(5): 47–48.

Zippo, Mary, and Greenberg, Karen. November/December 1982. "Roundup." *Personnel* 59(6): 52–53.

Zippo, Mary, and Northart, Pamela. 1983. "Review of 'The Employment Interview: A Social Judgment Process,' by Edward C. Webster, S.I.P. Publications, 1982." *Personnel* 60(1): 79.

INDEX

A

AAC (see Association of American Colleges)
AAUP (see American Association of University Professors)
Academe, 82
Academic rank
 salary differences, 23
 sex discriminaton, 44
 women, 24
Academic staffing, 24, 81
Academy of Educational Development (AED), 28
ACE (see American Council on Education)
Accounting
 faculty salary, 24
 part-time faculty use, 25
ACHE (see Association for Continuing Higher Education)
"Acting" positions, 6
Administrators
 desired attributes, 53–63
 handbook on selection, 1
 organizational fit, 9
 selection, 5–8
 women and minority groups, 42, 48
Advertisements (see Posting positions)
AED (see Academy of Educational Development)
Affirmative action
 director responsibility, 47, 81
 enforcement/litigation, 43–46
 job posting, 17
 policies/procedures, 46–47
 statistics, 41–43
African American Institute, 22
AGB (see Association of Governing Boards of Universities and
 Colleges)
Allied health fields: faculty rank, 23
Alton, Bruce, 27
Alumni director, 63
American Association of University Professors (AAUP), 14, 82
American Council on Education (ACE), 1, 16
American Psychological Association (APA), 22
American Society for Personnel Administrators, 73, 81
Amherst College: search boycott, 13
APA (see American Psychological Association)
Applications: recordkeeping, 15
Asians, enrollment, 49
Association for Continuing Higher Education (ACHE), 17
Association of American Colleges (AAC), 27

International Association of Universities, 17
Internships, 51
Interpersonal skills, 54–55
Interviews
     conducting, 75–79
     consultant role, 30
     interviewer responsibility, 75
     objectives, 74
     screening procedures, 18–20
     selection method, 73–74
     structure, 74–75
     validity, 73

J

Journals
     job posting, 17, 22
     personnel selection guides, 81

K

Kauffman, Joseph, 28
Korn-Ferry, 28

L

Leadership
     interpersonal skills, 54
     presidential, 55–57
     "right," 53–54
Leaks
     affirmative action, 47
     confidential search, 39
Legitimacy of appointments, 5
Letters of reference, 65–66
Litigation: affirmative action, 44–45
Logs of applications/actions, 15

M

McCarthy era, 37
McKnight Foundation, 50
Management skills, 60
Massachusetts Institute of Technology: black staff, 41
Mathematics faculty use, 25
Meetings: professional, 22
Mentors, 49, 51
Michigan: minority doctoral fellowships, 50
Minority Academic Careers Program, 50

P

Participatory management, 8
Personnel office, 81–83
"Personnelite" (newsletter), 17
Planning skills, 59
Political factors
    candidate selection, 86
    favorite candidates, 12
    leaks, 39
    public institutions, 14
Posting positions, 6, 16–18, 22
Powell, Lewis F., Jr., 45
Presidency
    affirmative action commitment, 47
    "builder," 53
    internal vs. external candidates, 7, 8
    job posting, 6
    leadership, 55–57
    preferred attributes, 9, 54–55, 58
    presidential team, 63
    public knowledge of candidacy, 36
    search process, 5
    spouses, 57
Presidential assistants, 62
Presidential Search Consultation Service (PSCS), 27, 33
Press: leak possibilities, 39
Private institutions
    high demand faculty, 24
    presidential leadership qualities, 55
    search committee size, 12
    women administrators, 42
Private sector salary competition, 24
Professional development programs, 50
Promoting from within (see Candidates/internal)
Provosts
    affirmative action commitment, 47
    internal candidates, 7
PSCS (see Presidential Search Consultation Service)
Public institutions
    affirmative action, 41
    high demand faculty, 24
    openness and disclosure, 35–36
    political factors, 14
    search committee size, 12

Q

Qualifications, 53–63

R

ASHE-ERIC HIGHER EDUCATION REPORTS

Starting in 1983, the Association for the Study of Higher Education assumed cosponsorship of the Higher Education Reports with the ERIC Clearinghouse on Higher Education. For the previous 11 years, ERIC and the American Association for Higher Education prepared and published the reports.

Each report is the definitive analysis of a tough higher education problem, based on a thorough research of pertinent literature and institutional experiences. Report topics, identified by a national survey, are written by noted practitioners and scholars with prepublication manuscript reviews by experts.

Eight monographs (10 monographs before 1985) in the ASHE-ERIC Higher Education Report series are published each year, available individually or by subscription. Subscription to eight issues is $60 regular; $50 for members of AERA, AAHE, and AIR; $40 for members of ASHE. (Add $7.50 outside the United States.)

Prices for single copies, including 4th class postage and handling, are $10.00 regular and $7.50 for members of AERA, AAHE, AIR, and ASHE ($7.50 regular and $6.00 for members for 1983 and 1984 reports, $6.50 regular and $5.00 for members for reports published before 1983). If faster 1st class postage is desired for U.S. and Canadian orders, add $.75 for each publication ordered; overseas, add $4.50. For VISA and MasterCard payments, include card number, expiration date, and signature. Orders under $25 must be prepaid. Bulk discounts are available on orders of 15 or more reports (not applicable to subscriptions). Order from the Publications Department, Association for the Study of Higher Education, One Dupont Circle, Suite 630, Washington, D.C. 20036, 202/296-2597. Write for a publication list of all the Higher Education Reports available.

1986 Higher Education Reports

1. Post-tenure Faculty Evaluation: Threat or Opportunity?
   Christine M. Licata

2. Blue Ribbon Commissions and Higher Education: Changing Academe from the Outside
   Janet R. Johnson and Laurence R. Marcus

3. Responsive Professional Education: Balancing Outcomes and Opportunities
   Joan S. Stark, Malcolm A. Lowther, and Bonnie M.K. Hagerty

4. Increasing Students' Learning: A Faculty Guide to Reducing Stress among Students
   Neal A. Whitman, David C. Spendlove, and Claire H. Clark

5. Student Financial Aid and Women: Equity Dilemma?
   Mary Moran

6. The Master's Degree: Tradition, Diversity, Innovation
   Judith S. Glazer

7. The College, the Constitution, and the Consumer Student: Implications for Policy and Practice
   Robert M. Hendrickson and Annette Gibbs

8. Selecting College and University Personnel: The Quest and the Questions
   Richard A. Kaplowitz

Selecting College and University Personnel

1985 Higher Education Reports

1. Flexibility in Academic Staffing: Effective Policies and Practices
   Kenneth P. Mortimer, Marque Bagshaw, and Andrew T. Masland

2. Associations in Action: The Washington, D.C., Higher
   Education Community
   Harland G. Bloland

3. And on the Seventh Day: Faculty Consulting and Supplemental
   Income
   Carol M. Boyer and Darrell R. Lewis

4. Faculty Research Performance: Lessons from the Sciences and
   Social Sciences
   John W. Creswell

5. Academic Program Reviews: Institutional Approaches, Expectations,
   and Controversies
   Clifton F. Conrad and Richard F. Wilson

6. Students in Urban Settings: Achieving the Baccalaureate Degree
   Richard C. Richardson, Jr., and Louis W. Bender

7. Serving More Than Students: A Critical Need for College Student
   Personnel Services
   Peter H. Garland

8. Faculty Participation in Decision Making: Necessity or Luxury?
   Carol E. Floyd

1984 Higher Education Reports

1. Adult Learning: State Policies and Institutional Practices
   K. Patricia Cross and Anne-Marie McCartan

2. Student Stress: Effects and Solutions
   Neal A. Whitman, David C. Spendlove, and Claire H. Clark

3. Part-time Faculty: Higher Education at a Crossroads
   Judith M. Gappa

4. Sex Discrimination Law in Higher Education: The Lessons of the
   Past Decade
   *J. Ralph Lindgren, Patti T. Ota, Perry A. Zirkel, and
   Nan Van Gieson*

5. Faculty Freedoms and Institutional Accountability: Interactions and
   Conflicts
   Steven G. Olswang and Barbara A. Lee

6. The High-Technology Connection: Academic/Industrial Cooperation
   for Economic Growth
   Lynn G. Johnson

7. Employee Educational Programs: Implications for Industry and
   Higher Education
   Suzanne W. Morse

8. Academic Libraries: The Changing Knowledge Centers of Colleges
   and Universities
   Barbara B. Moran

9. Futures Research and the Strategic Planning Process: Implications for Higher Education
   James L. Morrison, William L. Renfro, and Wayne I. Boucher

10. Faculty Workload: Research, Theory, and Interpretation
    Harold E. Yuker

1983 Higher Education Reports

1. The Path to Excellence: Quality Assurance in Higher Education
   Laurence R. Marcus, Anita O. Leone, and Edward D. Goldberg

2. Faculty Recruitment, Retention, and Fair Employment: Obligations and Opportunities
   John S. Waggaman

3. Meeting the Challenges: Developing Faculty Careers
   Michael C. T. Brookes and Katherine L. German

4. Raising Academic Standards: A Guide to Learning Improvement
   Ruth Talbott Keimig

5. Serving Learners at a Distance: A Guide to Program Practices
   Charles E. Feasley

6. Competence, Admissions, and Articulation: Returning to the Basics in Higher Education
   Jean L. Preer

7. Public Service in Higher Education: Practices and Priorities
   Patricia H. Crosson

8. Academic Employment and Retrenchment: Judicial Review and Administrative Action
   Robert M. Hendrickson and Barbara A. Lee

9. Burnout: The New Academic Disease
   Winifred Albizu Meléndez and Rafael M. de Guzmán

10. Academic Workplace: New Demands, Heightened Tensions
    Ann E. Austin and Zelda F. Gamson

NOTES

NOTES

Quantity		Amount

_____ Please enter my subscription to the 1986 ASHE-ERIC Higher Education Reports at $60.00, 25% off the cover price. _____

_____ Please enter my subscription to the 1987 Higher Education Reports at $60.00 _____

I certify that I am a member of AAHE, AERA, or AIR (circle one) and qualify for the special rate of $50.00.

_____ 1986 series subscription _____
_____ 1987 series subscription _____

I certify that I am a member of ASHE and qualify for the special rate of $40.00.

_____ 1986 series subscription _____
_____ 1987 series subscription _____

Individual reports are available at the following prices:
1985 and forward, $10.00 each ($7.50 for members).
1983 and 1984, $7.50 each ($6.00 for members).
1982 and back, $6.50 each ($5.00 for members).

Please send me the following reports:

_____
(Title)

_____ Report No. ____ ( ) _____
_____ Report No. ____ ( ) _____
_____ Report No. ____ ( ) _____

SUBTOTAL: _____
Optional 1st Class Shipping ($.75 per book) _____
TOTAL AMOUNT DUE: _____

NOTE: All prices subject to change.

Name _____
Title _____
Inst. _____
Addr. _____
_____
City _____ ST _____ Zip _____
Phone _____
Signature _____
☐ Check enclosed, payable to ASHE.
☐ Please charge my credit card:
     ☐ Visa ☐ MasterCard (check one)

☐☐☐☐ ☐☐☐☐ ☐☐☐☐ ☐☐☐☐

Expiration date _____

ASHE ERIC®

Association for the Study of Higher Education
The George Washington University
One Dupont Circle, Suite 630, Dept. E
Washington, D.C. 20036
Phone: (202) 296-2597

Did you remember:
1. To enclose your method of payment?
2. To indicate clearly which reports you wanted?
3. To sign and date your check?
4. To put postage on this card?

Thank you for your order. Please allow 3–4 weeks for delivery.

Please fold along dotted line and staple close

FROM: _____
       _____
       _____
       _____

**Association for the Study of Higher Education
One Dupont Circle, Suite 630, Dept. E
Washington, DC 20036**